A NECESSARY
Evil

A NECESSARY
Evil

Managing Employee Activity
on Facebook, Twitter, LinkedIn...
and the Hundreds of Other Social Media Sites

ALIAH D. WRIGHT

FOREWORD BY HENRY G. "HANK" JACKSON, CEO, SHRM

Society for Human Resource Management
Alexandria, Virginia
www.shrm.org

Strategic Human Resource Management India
Mumbai, India
www.shrmindia.org

Society for Human Resource Management
Haidian District Beijing, China
www.shrm.org/cn

The Society for Human Resource Management (SHRM) is the world's largest association devoted to human resource management. Representing more than 250,000 members in over 140 countries, the Society serves the needs of HR professionals and advances the interests of the HR profession. Founded in 1948, SHRM has more than 575 affiliated chapters within the United States and subsidiary offices in China and India. Visit SHRM online at www.shrm.org.

Interior Design: Auburn Associates, Inc.
Cover Design: Bravery Corporation
Author Photo by: Christine Chong

Library of Congress Cataloging-in-Publication Data
Wright, Aliah D., 1968-
  Social media at work / Aliah D. Wright.
      pages   cm
  Includes bibliographical references and index.
  ISBN 978-1-58644-341-2
1. Personal Internet use in the workplace. 2. Social media. 3. Personnel management.
4. Information technology—Management. I. Title.
  HF5549.5.P39W75 2013
  302.23′1—dc23

                                                              2013008129
                                                              13-0214

Contents

For my son, Jaden Christopher,
and my best friend, Patrick N. Foster

Acknowledgments

B efore I thank anyone, I have to thank God because with Him all things are possible—including the ability to write what is essentially a textbook in less than a year.

There are many people I'd like to thank for their inspiration and encouragement. They include the book's publisher and editor, Christopher Anzalone, and the book's content editor, the Society for Human Resource Management's Director of Social Strategy and Engagement Curtis Midkiff. Both were incredibly supportive, and their beliefs in my capabilities were simply transcendent.

I'd also like to thank my colleagues and friends: Desda Moss, Theresa Minton-Eversole, Allen Smith, Les Carr, SHRM's Manager, Social Networking & Online Communities Anne-Margaret Olsson, and SHRM Manager of Employment Wanda Barrett, who all read and weighed in on early drafts; my swell new supervisor, Beth Mirza; colleagues Rebecca Hastings, Gary Rubin, Leon Rubis, Steve Miller, Kathy Gurchiek, Bill Leonard, Steve Bates, Joanne Deschenaux, Roy Maurer, Gretchen Kraft, Howard Wallack, Christine Balch, Judit Slezak, and Renee Sumby, as well as SHRM Librarian Montrese Hamilton; SHRM's entire public relations department, but especially Amy Thompson, Mary Kaylor, Jennifer Hughes, Julie Malveaux, and Ciara Calbert; and Andi Cale and Vincent Caldwell of the SHRMStore for giving me all kinds of books. I have to thank my very good friends Norris Benns, Stephanie Touissant, and Sylvia Rainford; the authors and writers K. Reid, Saadia Ahmed, Greg Wright, and Greg Barrett for their inspiration and support, including good friend *Time* magazine Senior Editor Tatsha Robertson; and the members of the Writers and Authors Collective Group I started on Facebook. I'd like to thank, too, the many HR professionals and social media gurus who contributed their expertise about social media, including Gerry Crispin, Buzz Rooney, Jay Kuhns, Sean Charles, Geoff Webb, Laurie Ruettimann, Damon Lovett,

Eric B. Meyer, Jessica Miller-Merrell, Craig Fisher, Yvette Cameron, Brad Warga, Jessica Lee, China Miner Gorman, Paul Smith, Michael Schmidt, Kyle Cartier, Bruce Kneuer, Ryan Estis, Lars Schmidt, Joey V. Price, John Hagel, and the many, many other people who let me tap their collective knowledge to bring you this book.

Note: In addition to relying on her own professional expertise and research, the author has incorporated existing SHRM Online *content in the development of this book.*

Foreword

Every generation faces the same challenge: the ongoing, and sometimes relentless, pace of change. Usually, the younger generation is the agent of that change—prodding older generations into acceptance and accommodation. Then that generation eventually looks up and suddenly sees an *oncoming* generation doing the same thing, pushing for new changes and developments.

It's just the natural order, and it's positive. It brings discovery and enlightenment, exciting new ways of getting things done, and rewarding and enriching new ways of valuing and utilizing the *differences* of people around the world.

Fortunately, both the young and the not-so-young are blessed with the interpretive talents of researchers, writers, and emerging thought leaders like Aliah Wright. With her wit and bright tone, she guides us all through the main highways and side streets of the most important pathway of change since the birth of the digital era—the phenomenon of social media. *A Necessary Evil: Managing Employee Activity on Facebook, Twitter, LinkedIn … and the Hundreds of Other Social Media Sites* is a necessary roadmap, whether we are just starting the journey or learning to master it.

At the Society for Human Resource Management, we remind our members that change is always present—whether it comes from new government laws and regulations, or from innovative competition in an expanding global economy. The message is simple: Adapt or risk becoming irrelevant.

So, also goes the gospel for the reality of social media. It's not a fad destined to fade away. It has proven itself to be truly transformative, part of a technological and social revolution. It can streamline communications, affect markets, and help foster engaged employees, and even boost the bottom line!

Employers and employees alike must understand the distinct possibilities and effects of social media. For instance, employers must develop balanced social media policies that encourage open communication while still protecting the organization's brand.

Employees need to appreciate that what's posted is permanent, and that there are no real secrets. Social messaging has the potential to improve the quality of life, but it can also affect livelihoods and career opportunities.

As Aliah writes in the following pages, "change is never easy." But thanks to navigators and translators like Aliah, we *do* know what it is. And we know how to make it work for us. As she states, all we need to do is "embrace it."

Henry G. "Hank" Jackson, CPA, is president and CEO of the Society for Human Resource Management, the world's largest organization devoted to human resources.

1 | It's *Social* Media: Forget Control, Adopt Integration

She walks into your office and hands you a sheet of paper. It is a printout of a colleague's Facebook status update. It reads:

"This place is a hellhole. If I had a car today I would up and quit."

The above post is a real Facebook status update taken from a discussion on HR Talk, the Society for Human Resource Management's bulletin board.[2] The question posed was: "What should be the next step for the manager? Discussion? Termination? Nothing?"

Good question. Employers are responding in myriad ways to the things their employees do on social networking sites—after the fact.

Consider these real-life scenarios:

1. HMV, an entertainment retailer in Britain, laid off nearly 200 employees on January 31, 2013. Someone on the company's social media team used the Twitter account to send out this tweet:

"We're tweeting live from HR where we're all being fired! Exciting!! #hmvXFactorFiring."[3] Within 30 minutes that tweet had gone viral, and several other people within the company began tweeting about the mass terminations. Another tweet followed:

"Just overheard our Marketing Director (he's staying, folks) ask 'How do I shut down Twitter?'" #hmvXFactorFiring."

2. In another case, "an employee . . . decided that she was going to take a picture of a co-worker's cubicle" and post it "to her Facebook page with a status like 'slob' or something along those lines," Janine Truitt, senior HR representative at Brookhaven National Laboratory said of an incident relayed to her. The woman "was friends with a few of the clients of this company and they saw the picture and commented. It became a joke online [until] one of those clients print-screened the page and sent it to her boss." The woman who posted the photo was fired, and "two other employees were cited for similar derogatory writing on [the Facebook post]," Truitt said.[4]

3. Shortly after President Barack Obama was elected, the president's then-chief speechwriter, 27-year-old Jon Favreau, was seen in a Facebook photo groping a cardboard cutout of newly appointed Secretary of State Hillary Rodham Clinton as someone else placed a bottle of beer to her lips.[5] Favreau apologized and kept his position until he resigned in March 2013.

4. Who could forget the infamous "Cisco Fatty" tweet?

In 2009, 22-year-old Connor Riley reportedly tweeted this to the world: "Cisco just offered me a job! Now I have to weigh the utility of a fatty paycheck against the daily commute to San Jose and hating the work."[6]

Afterward Tim Levad, who was affiliated with Cisco, fired back:

"Who is the hiring manager? I'm sure they would love to know that you will hate the work. We here at Cisco are versed in the web."

Riley did not get the job.

5. Sergeant. Gary Stein, a nine-year military veteran was cited for misconduct and a military panel suggested he be dishonorably discharged and lose his pension and security clearance for posting disparaging comments about President Obama on his Facebook page.[7]

6. Dr. June Talvitie-Siple lost her $92,000-a-year job as a high-school supervisor for math and science in Cohasset, Massachusetts, after parents found comments on her Facebook page referring to students as "germ bags" and town residents as "arrogant and snobby."[8]

Now, let's say for example, some employees you supervise go on Facebook on their own time and disparage your company publicly in a profane manner and the post goes viral.

The ensuing publicity creates a firestorm, and it is a huge disaster for your firm. Your CEO walks into your office and demands to know whether you can fire these people.

What do you say? Do you know anything about labor relations law and whether employees' have the right to have discussions about work on the Internet—whether they are in the office or at home? Do you have a social media policy? Most companies do not. In fact, research from SHRM in 2011 revealed that companies with 99 or fewer employees were less likely to have a policy compared with organizations with 100 or more employees.[9]

As a manager, you need to get in front of situations like this *before* they happen and *before* they ruin your company's reputation (or cost you *your* job). In the case of HMV, perhaps confiscating the password to the company's main social media accounts and acting with transparency about pending layoffs could have averted the social media firestorm, which obviously ensued because the employees were shocked to find out they were being let go.

The days of employers controlling the message are gone—in HMV's case, however, the employer could have softened the blow by trusting its employees with the news of the impending layoffs before the last possible moment, especially given the company had been having financial problems.

Now, let's take a look at the case of American Medical Response of Connecticut Inc.

In 2010 the National Labor Relations Board (NLRB)—a federal agency that protects the rights of employees to organize to better their working conditions and pay—issued a complaint against American Medical Response after it fired an employee[10] who used her home computer to post a profanity-laced tirade about her supervisor on her personal Facebook page (the post included comments from some of her co-workers).[11] It was quickly dubbed "the Facebook Firing Case" by the press. The NLRB for the first time found that an employee's Facebook posts were protected speech, meaning employees have the right to complain about working conditions—even online.[12] It also found that the company's blogging and Internet posting policy had illegal guidelines—including one that kept employees from making disparaging comments when talking about their organization or its supervisors and another that prohibited employees from depicting the company in any way over the Internet without company permission.

There are dozens of stories like these—real stories—of employees engaging in odd or egregious behavior on social networking sites, so many in fact, we could fill an entire book about them. How are business leaders, managers, and HR professionals handling situations like these? Some are handling them as they appear—on a case-by-case basis. Others are following policies they have instituted and are consulting attorneys or ignoring them altogether.

What is right? What is wrong?

As a reporter and editor for *SHRM Online* and *HR Magazine*, publications of the Society for Human Resource Management (SHRM), an organization dedicated to assisting human resource professionals, I have witnessed the birth of social media and the ever-evolving use of social networking. I have been adventurous in my career as an editor and reporter. It was in that spirit that I hopped on Twitter in 2009 when the former chief operating officer of SHRM, China Gorman, went on the site to engage HR professionals. I, too, was leery at first (especially about putting my profile on LinkedIn) and then venturing on to Facebook and just about every other social networking site mentioned in this book. As a social media "lurker" initially, and then an active contributor, I have watched in fascination at the power social media has to transform lives. I have also learned a lot, too—and as journalist, one of the things I love about my career is how much I have learned through social interactions—on and off the web. My colleagues and I have spoken to hundreds of HR professionals—experts and novices of social media who are curious, concerned, and enthralled by the ability this new communication mechanism possesses to change and enhance lives. Yet, too many companies, whether from fear, confusion, or a stubborn inability to embrace change, are continuing to ban employee use of what has essentially become our new telephone.

It is my hope that this book—which draws from dozens of interviews, research, and best practices of HR professionals operating within the social realm—will provide guidance on how to handle bad situations—hopefully before they occur. But as managers, to do that you must understand how social media works, how it has changed the landscape of the professional work environment, which networks employees are using, how they are using them, how often, and when (basically 24/7).

Good companies pay attention to the social networking sites their customers and employees inhabit. They watch their behaviors; they listen to their concerns; they apologize when their companies make mistakes; they are transparent and honest; and they engage their audiences and employees to foster growth, increase brand awareness, and tap their collective knowledge to improve their bottom lines.

If you are unaware of how social networking sites operate, what their culture is like, and how people behave on these sites, your employees' activities there may affect your company in any number of ways. Can employees really write whatever they want on a social networking site? (Um, yes). Should they? Are they entitled to privacy on social networking sites—whether they are engaging in social media activities while at work or on weekends, on their own devices? How private is private when it is shared with 250 "friends?" What is HR to do?

As social media continues its metamorphosis, employers must have a grasp on its uses, not just within the social realm, but within the business context as well. Social media is not a waste of time or a fad. It can enhance business strategy and provide analytics to foster corporate growth and development as well as help employees find solutions and come up with innovative ideas—even as they network with colleagues, peers, and "friends."

Anyone who manages employees who access social media from the palms of their hands must stay abreast of the constantly shifting ways social media does all these things while helping employees maintain productivity and avoid damaging reputations. In addition, managers must help employees be mindful of corporate values while safeguarding corporate data. *This resource will help managers guide employees in their use of such sites while balancing productivity and will help HR professionals set policies that do both.*

Change is never easy. Yet we live in a world that is changing every single day. Social media is a new ever evolving tool that can help expand our knowledge and our reach and help us innovate and collaborate in bold, new ways.

Embrace it.

*"How do you pay attention to your kids or your career if you're not on
LinkedIn or Facebook? It's almost like you're saying 'I'm going to stay
stuck in the dark ages while everybody else is going through a stage of
enlightenment.'"*

—Laurie Ruettimann, HR consultant

2 | What *Is* Social Media?

It's Facebook. It's Twitter. It's LinkedIn. It's Google's Blogger and Google+, YouTube, and niche site SHRM Connect. It's Instagram and Pinterest. It's Quora and GetGlue. It's Foursquare, Myspace (yes, people are *still* using it), Imgur, Fancy, Reddit, Yammer, Chatter, Posterous, Path, Second Life, Letterboxd, Viddy, and now the many games through Zynga.

It's deviantART, LiveJournal, Tagged, Orkut, CafeMom, Ning, Meetup, myLife, myYearbook, and Badoo. Even Pandora has a social networking component. Social media is niche communities of practice where doctors, scientists, technophobes, youngsters, singletons, Boomers, and Millennials are congregating to share, engage, meet, and innovate online. It is also podcasting and the many blog sites like Tumblr, Blogger, Wordpress, and Storify.

This list is not conclusive or exhaustive—not by any means. New social sites appear seemingly every day. Social media is any website or mobile application ("app") that allows people to connect and engage others in direct dialogue—without editorial filters—a scary concept for most corporations fearful that employees will damage their brands. For HR professionals and people managers everywhere it can either be a bane to their existence or a really, really cool collaboration tool.

Social media is, in a nutshell, content generated by online users. It is back-and-forth communication. It's engaging with people, whether near or far, in ways that have never been done before. It's pervasive and invasive. But more important is that it's not going anywhere.

NEWS FLASH: THIS IS THE WAY WE COMMUNICATE. GET OVER IT

Let's face it. Your employees are already on Facebook, Google Blogger, Twitter, LinkedIn, Flickr, and Google + and will most certainly be on whatever shiny, new social network that has not been developed yet but will probably be just as hip and exciting. They are adding their comments and expressing their opinions under articles and blogs and in other forums as well. They are not using their desktop computers, either. Most are deploying social media from an iPhone, iPad, BlackBerry, Android, Windows Phone, Kindle Fire, or other device. They are using it in their cars (hopefully not while driving), under their desks, and in the bathroom.

"If employees can't access social media, they're cut off from their peers and the news. It's isolating and unrealistic," Raleigh, North Carolina-based HR consultant Laurie Ruettimann told me during an interview. "Your employees are not robots. They don't show up 9 to 5 and just work. They bring their lives in with them and you want them to go out externally and understand what's happening in the world and bring that back into your workforce," she said. Social media does just that.

So forget about stopping them from chatting on Facebook, huddling on Google, tweeting, or playing Angry Birds, FarmVille, Scramble, Draw Something, or Words with Friends. All of the sites have become so tightly woven into our lives with more than a billion people using them that expecting employees to curtail these activities at work— particularly members of Generation Y, who have grown up working and playing (otherwise known as multitasking)—is futile at best and most likely unrealistic.

Consider Cisco's 2012 Connected Word Technology report. In a news release, Cisco stated that

> "while two out of five [respondents] said their company's policy forbids them to use company-issued devices for non-work activities, nearly three out of four (71 percent) said they don't always obey those policies.
>
> The craving to stay connected means that the lines between work and social life/family life are blurring. People check for work updates and communicate at all hours from every place imaginable. *Time is elastic: For Generation Y there are no clear markers between the workday and personal time—both blend and overlap throughout the day and night.*"[1]

In fact, some studies show job candidates trust companies more when they are allowed to use social media. "Within those companies that successfully use internal social media tools (Yammer, Chatter, etc.), employees are 60 percent more likely to give their employer the benefit of the doubt during a crisis, 67 percent more likely to support government policies that their company supports, and 39 percent more likely to recommend their company's products and services to friends and family members outside of the company. In general, we're seeing in our research that social media can be a powerful tool for empowering employees to become eager and proactive brand ambassadors willing to share ownership of their company's reputation," Scott Healy, a researcher with Gagen MacDonald, wrote in January 2013. Healy also shared his research with me for the book.[2]

No one is advocating letting employees run wild, however—quite the opposite. There are rules. Of course there are rules! You are in charge, after all. Laying out the ground rules will help you help employees be productive and engaged. But you have to use the tools to know how they work.

As NPR senior director of talent acquisition & innovation Lars Schmidt told me during an interview, "social media allows you the ability to watch and observe thought leaders who are present in the space and see what they're reading, sharing, discussing, and see who they're interacting with." It's a window into a world of information unlike any other. It gives HR professionals the opportunity to connect with peers "in any field in any region throughout the world," Schmidt added. "Social media is the great enabler of communication."

As a social media advocate, journalist, and student and a power user of these tools, my goal is to inform executives, HR professionals, hiring managers, and supervisors of the benefits of allowing employees to use social media and to walk away with realistic expectations. Job performance will not be thrown out the window. Rather, this approach requires trust and transparency—from the worker and the employer.

After all, you are not hiring stupid people. So why treat them like nitwits after you have given them jobs?

There are more than 7 billion people in the world, and more than 2.4 billion of them used the Internet worldwide. Moreover, Nielsen reports that Americans spend more time on Facebook than on any other website on the Internet.[3] Google's Blogger comes in second, and Twitter comes in third.[4] One study reported social media was harder to resist than sex![5] Statistics show that one out of every seven minutes spent online is spent on Facebook, which reports that most of its users access the site from the palms of their hands.[6] Little wonder, according to Reston, Virginia-based comScore.com, as of June 2011, 78.5 million Americans owned smartphones, and Portio Research's *Mobile Factbook 2012* reports that at the end of 2011, there were nearly 6 billion mobile subscribers globally and predicts that number to grow to more than 8 billion by the end of 2016, meaning there will be more mobile phone subscriptions than there are people worldwide.[7]

Think back to 2005. That year, most people went online to surf the web, shop, and e-mail each other. Today, nearly 2 billion worldwide are accessing social media sites. But back then, companies used their websites for "corporate communication, product promotion, customer service, and, in some cases, e-commerce. Relatively few people were members of online communities," McKinsey pointed out in a 2012 study. "Social networking sites were for college students; and chief marketing officers did not worry about how many online fans 'liked' their company's products."[8]

Telligent, a social networking site for corporations, reported in 2012 that people spend a quarter of their time online on social networking sites.[9] According to Experian's *The 2012 Digital Marketer: Benchmark and Trend Report*, 91 percent of adults used social media regularly in December 2011.[10] More businesses are now turning to social networks to keep up with clients, customers, and their employees.

In May 2012, Google and London-based marketing and research group Millward Brown commissioned the study *How Social Technologies Drive Business Success*.[11] The international study found that 69 percent of 2,700 professionals in the United Kingdom, France, Germany, Italy, the Netherlands, Spain, and Sweden predict that businesses that embrace social networking tools will grow faster than those that do not, and 53 percent believe those that do not embrace social media will not be around to discuss it.

Gagen MacDonald reported in December 2011 that 51 percent of employees polled said their companies use social media tools within their firms, and studies show that employees have more confidence in companies that use such tools to help them collaborate and solve core business problems.[12] Yet, according to SHRM 2011 research, 43 percent of organizations blocked access to social media platforms on organization-owned computers or handheld devices even though 68 percent of those organizations reported they currently use social media to reach external audiences.[13]

What's more, the use of such sites is growing across all age groups—including the workforce of the future. According to a 2012 study by the Pew Internet & American Life Project, half of adults and three-quarters of teenagers in America use social networking sites—most of them are on Facebook.[14]

This is the way we communicate now. There is no going back.

As of December 2012, Facebook was the largest social networking site in the world with more than a billion monthly active users, according to its website.[15] Facebook went public in spring of 2012. In October of 2012, website analytics firm Alexa reported that Facebook was "the most popular site in the world . . . search engines refer approximately 5 percent of visits to it."[16]

Alexa reported that, on average, users typically visit Facebook for "roughly 25 minutes, with 48 seconds spent on each page view. Relative to the overall population of Internet users, this site's audience tends to be users who browse from school and home; they are also disproportionately women."[17]

Founded in February 2004 by one of Harvard's most successful college dropouts, Mark Zuckerberg, the company's growth has exploded with a reach into nearly every country on this planet.

In May 2012 the *Los Angeles Times* reported that teenagers were abandoning the popular site for Tumblr, Twitter, Instagram, and Google + and texting each other on cell phones.[18] But as the Pew study mentioned earlier states: "We found no evidence among our sample that length of time using Facebook is associated with a decline in Facebook activity. On the contrary, the more time that has passed since a user started using Facebook, the more frequently he/she makes status updates, uses the 'like' button, comments on friends' content, and tags friends in photos."[19]

Meanwhile, "we continue to focus on growing our user base across all geographies, including relatively less-penetrated, large markets such as Brazil, Germany, India, Japan, Russia, and South Korea," Facebook stated in the U.S. Securities and Exchange Commission (SEC) filing, which also revealed that as of March 31, 2012, more than 125 billion friend connections were on Facebook.[20] According to its website, approximately 80 percent of its monthly active users are outside the U.S. and Canada, and approximately 526 million daily active users visited the site in March 2012; 488 million people used Facebook mobile products in March 2012, and the site had more than 500 million mobile monthly active users as of April 20, 2012.

The site has changed the ways in which we live and communicate with one another.

WE'RE NOT ANONYMOUS ANYMORE, BUT SOMETIMES WE ACT LIKE IT

Once upon a time, when the Internet was new and there was no such thing as Facebook, and the concept of transparent and honest was not a concept, people spent time anonymously chatting with strangers in chat rooms, posting snarky comments on blogs and newspaper sites, and behaving in ways that would make a grandmother blush and say hush. (Guess what? They still do). But technology evolved, and so, too, did behaviors—for some people. Technological advancements have forever changed the ways in which we interact with one another, and lots of research has been conducted about the nature of online behavior when anonymity is involved.[21] The computer screen allows some of us to abandon courteous behaviors as well as social conventions and inhibitions online. People become made-up user-names and avatars. Some become more provocative. It is easier to be vitriolic if the object of our dialogue is not face-to-face.

But Facebook changed all that. People began connecting with friends, co-workers, ex-loves, former colleagues, classmates, teachers, coaches, and family. But every now and then, they continue to leave common sense and social conventions behind—forgetting now that their real names, photos, and reputations are attached.

Briefly consider the case of Adria Richards. In March 2013, Richards was reportedly attending a technology convention in California when she became offended because two men seated behind her made what she deemed sexists remarks. But instead of turning around and speaking to them, switching seats, or physical getting up to report them to conference staff, she decided to alert conference organizers in a different way. She took the photo of those who had offended her and tweeted:[22]

Source: Adria Richards Tweet https://twitter.com/adriarichards/status/3134176558 79102464

Not only was one of the men reportedly fired, but Richards' tweet caused a worldwide media hailstorm, and she lost her job. The CEO of her firm, SendGrid, wrote on the corporate blog:

"To be clear, SendGrid supports the right to report inappropriate behavior, whenever and wherever it occurs. What we do not support was how she reported the conduct. Her decision to tweet the comments and photographs of the people who made the comments crossed the line. Publicly shaming the offenders—and bystanders—was not the appropriate way to handle the situation."[23]

Richards may have felt she was right. But it doesn't matter. It is discourteous to take someone's photo and publish it online with disparaging (venturing on defamatory) comments without their permission or consent. People do it every day, but that does not make it right. More people should think critically before posting something in anger online, for a lot of reasons.

Some people share the most intimate details of their lives on Facebook, which has caused many to fiercely protect the data that live there. Social media engagement can be a both a goldmine and landmine for employers—those seeking information and those exposed to more information than necessary.

Of course, the key to using Facebook and any social networking site mentioned in this book effectively lies in actually reading the primers contained within the site's Help Centers, FAQs (frequently asked questions), or About sections. I am not going to delve into a lot of explanation on how to do that. If you can read this book, you can read Facebook's privacy settings. Let me say that again. Read Facebook's privacy settings, and go over them often because Facebook changes those settings often. Adjusting privacy settings is critical, and paying attention to how your friends' privacy settings are set is important as well. Many social networking sites' default setting is public, and users may have to change their settings to privatize them.

Users especially need to be mindful of this: *Anything posted to a social networking site can be seen by anyone at any time—regardless of a person's privacy settings*, as seen in the preface to this book and the following cartoon. "Choosing how your information is going to be disseminated is key," HR blogger Michael Long, founder of the theredrecruiter.com, said when I interviewed him back in 2009.[24] If you do not want it out there, do not put it out there. "There's no real cure for stupid," he quipped. He added that employees (anyone, really) should exercise "common sense" when using Facebook or any other social networking site.

Fast Fact: Each and every single Tweet dating back to March 2006 is archived by the Library of Congress.

Of course, common sense is not common, and nothing ever really dies online.

In addition to the probability that your message may have been copied, retweeted, captured in a screenshot, printed out, e-mailed, or shared in some way, even if you deleted it, it is not really gone. It simply lives in a repository that the user cannot see but that the website host has kept in its database, ready to be accessed by the people who work and manage the content on that site, by hackers, or by law enforcement—Facebook's terms of service, notwithstanding.

TO FRIEND OR NOT TO FRIEND?

Perhaps you have seen the argument that people should be their true, authentic selves when engaging each other online—that behaving one way at work and another way in their personal lives is distracting. But this is the nature of human behavior, right? Few people behave in public the same way they do behind closed doors. But, more important, the reason why we have laws against discrimination is that people will always judge each other—whether we like it or not. We do not live in an ideal world. Not only what you publish on a social networking site or what is published about you could land you in hot water or distort someone's opinion of you. It could be what you like, want, or whom you befriend as well.

Consider these facts:

- In 2009 six people who worked for Hampton, Virginia, Sheriff B. J. Roberts were fired after they supported his re-election opponent. Specifically, Daniel Ray Carter was fired because he "liked" the Facebook page of Roberts' opponent. Facebook and the American Civil Liberties Union (ACLU) tried to sway the courts, saying a "like" was free speech. A federal judge disagreed, saying that merely liking a Facebook page does not warrant constitutional protection.[25]
- In 2009 Library of Congress employee Peter TerVeer "liked" the TwoDads.us Facebook page, a page that states it "promotes awareness of the gay and lesbian community." He claimed liking the page led to his boss discovering he was gay, which led to his dismissal.[26]
- In 2012 a Georgia police deputy was fired after he allegedly sent a Facebook friend request to a 23-year-old female prisoner.[27]

There are many, many reasons for and against friending colleagues. Being connected can foster more open communication. But it can potentially cause harm—not just from what you post on your timeline, but what the people you are connected to post and share about you as well—especially now that the "ticker" on the right side of the Facebook page can reveal items about others that used to be private.

In the years I have been covering technology for SHRM, and in the many years I have been on the sidelines of human behavior as a journalist, I have discovered one rule of thumb we should all live by: *If it is something that can be embarrassing or potentially lead to the loss of employment, do not put it on the Internet—even if you think no one who matters will see it.*

Let me reiterate it a different way. If the post, photo, or video is something you would not want the CEO of your company, your firm's legal counsel, or your grandmother to see, do *not* post it on a social networking site. And I hate to break it to you: Even if your birth name is not attached to your profile, your photos are. Your boss *still* knows what you look like.

We can all define friendship in varying degrees. However, recognize, too, that everyone is not your friend. Because of the personal nature of Facebook, many employment attorneys have advised employers to refrain from befriending colleagues or subordinates because they may be privy to information that may later prove discriminatory or that could show egregious behavior that could get the company sued. Or, again, as seen in the example in the preface to this book, you could get in hot water for sharing something with the wrong group of people.

"I just had a talk to my staff. I noticed one of our employees posted a "Good Morning!" on [Facebook] and a photo of her morning drive over the bridge—ON A HIGHWAY!!!!!! She is a wonderful person and I told her supervisor to explain the safety issues of texting and driving—much less taking a photo, posting to FB, and texting! I said that we need to approach this like drinking and driving—it is not safe for you, the other people on the road and is completely unacceptable for a responsible person to do. I want them to talk to her as a friend who cares about her future and as a fellow team member."

—Hellen Davis, CEO at Indaba Global Inc. and co-founder of the DISCflex assessment tools in Tampa and St. Petersburg[28]

So, should you connect with everyone?

Well, that is entirely up to you. There really is not a right or wrong answer to that question. It depends on how you choose to share information and with whom you choose to share it. This is a debate you can start on your own Facebook pages: We all behave in different ways around different people. It is why many people are more forthcoming with personal information on Facebook than they are on LinkedIn and why some people protect their Twitter updates and why others do not.

For example, before Kenexa was purchased by IBM, the company's social media manager, Bruce Kneuer, said in an interview for this book that he manages a number of Twitter accounts for Kenexa. One is @KenexaSocial. But he also has another Twitter account @BKneuer. The first account was where he shared business-related information. The second was his personal account, "where you can easily see what's of interest to me like education and technology. That's not a professional role."

He is not the only one. Thousands of people manage multiple accounts on various social networking sites—each representing personal and professional affiliations.

In winter of 2012, I posed this question to members of SHRM's official LinkedIn group: "Should You Friend Your Boss on Facebook?" Of those who responded, 92 percent said "no," and 7 percent said "yes." The comments were varied with quite a few people saying it depends on how you use Facebook (See Figure 2.1).

Figure 2.1   Should You Friend Your Boss on Facebook?

Comment from Michael Maggiotto Jr.:

One thing to remember is that there is a generational gap that must be considered. Many (and before someone chimes in to the contrary—many does not mean all) generation Y and younger live their lives rather loudly in social media. This means that things they enjoy doing . . . are available for the world to see. Some and I dare say many, of these images, stories, situations, et.al, can have a serious negative impact on their careers. If this is the case for you (you in the general sense, not addressing any specific person) then I would STRONGLY recommend NOT inviting anyone who may potentially be a professional connection to be a friend on Facebook or any other social media.

On the other hand, many generation X and older (and again, many does not mean all) do not live their lives nearly as loudly on social media. As such there is likely to be less content in their social media platforms and a lower likelihood that the boss or any other professional will find something that could be detrimental to their careers. If this is the case for you (and again, you in the general sense not addressing any specific person) then friending your boss or any other professional may not be as risky. But do not forget that they are friended and also be aware that they will be able to see [your posts and those that your friends post] so you may be held professionally accountable for the material that someone else in your circle of friends posts.

Right or wrong, that happens. Legal or not, that's reality. It is a battle that is currently being fought through the courts, but as we all know, the law lags technology. So, again, unless you have a strictly professional account on FB or other social media, I would advise not friending your boss or other professionals.

Comment from Dusty Tubbs:

Like most issues in life, it is not necessarily a clear yes or no question. Here in Hawaii we treat our co-workers as "ohana" (that means family in Hawaiian) and we probably form a closer bond than most corporate work places on the mainland. Since Facebook was designed to share information with your family/close friends (ohana) then "yes" it should be alright to share your Facebook pages with your co-workers and boss.

I think it would be appropriate for a middle manager to share Facebook pages with both managers above (where that person is aspiring to promote to) as well as with those below, that there is a closer bond/working relationship. Just like in the military . . . senior enlisted are connected with both the junior officer and the other enlisted.

Regardless of whom you share your Facebook pages with, a person should use some common sense in what they post. As long as you keep sensible friends, then you should also be safe. If a person is doing something that would disqualify them for a job, then perhaps they should not be doing it in the first place.

I control my Facebook [page] not because I am worried about somebody seeing something embarrassing about me, but rather as a form of protection. Identity thieves can learn enough about a person online to make stealing a person's identity too easy.

Prince Harry, I am sure, is not happy with his "naked" photos showing up on-line and in the tabloids. Perhaps he should have considered that before he took his clothes off. That is the point . . . don't do something that will embarrass you, or your family, and you will not have to worry about reading about it in public.

Perhaps the primary issue that most people forget about is that Facebook is not a "personal/private" website. Facebook is a public website! If you would not do something in front of your mother (or boss) then just do not do it at all, plain and simple.

Having said all of that, I also believe that Facebook is not a "professional" form of social media. Professionals use LinkedIn to share professional information. Rarely is there ever anything "inappropriate" placed on LinkedIn. In the rare instance when that does happen, it is taken down and the person that posted the inappropriate comment is warned not to do that again.

Regardless, every workplace should have a social media policy. Every employee (and potential employee) should be made to read, and sign a statement, stating they are aware of the company's policy and that failure to comply with it may lead to termination and/or the right to refuse employment.

Source: "Should You Friend Your Boss on Facebook?" SHRM Official Group LinkedIn Discussion, November, 2012. LinkedIn. www.linkedin.com/groupItem?view=&gid=42596 &type=member&item=180447631&qid=799894ae-5615-4b79-b0ec-0717ae40c40e& trk=group_search_item_list-0-b-ttl&go back=%2Eamf_42596_25011204. Comments used with permission.

One thing is certain, however. Social networking has allowed all of us a window into the lives of people we may never have connected with and to see the commonalities we all share in the interactions we have with our family and friends—especially on Facebook. It can be a bridge to building better relationships with people who are stakeholders or leaders or influencers. We can mine our social sites to share and broaden our knowledge and our influence. People connect with each other for different reasons, but those interactions can help foster collaboration and innovation while enhancing personal and professional relationships. Can you be too forthcoming? Certainly. Should you be? Of course not!

Now that Facebook has gone public, the rules presently surrounding the use of information stored on the site might change in the future. In fact, Facebook is notorious for changing things.

Think of Facebook as you would a party where only a select group of people get to share in your life, because it is *your* life. It is what you think, how you feel, and whom you are interacting with *and* what they think and what they feel. Remember the saying, "Beware of the company you keep"? Whether we like it or not, people make judgments about our behaviors and those of the people with whom we interact (that is why we have discrimination laws).

Nothing has changed, really—except the ways in which we communicate. And, as seen in Figure 2.2, more of us are starting to create and share content across various social networking sites.

We'll discuss social networks more in-depth in the resources guide at the end of this book. But, before we do that, let's take a look at influence.

The Power of Connections

Now we come to Klout and the power of connections.

Klout is not technically a social networking site, but it and the many other social connection-measurement sites like it claim they can measure social media influence. Those analytics are reportedly driving corporate behaviors. But what is Klout?

Well, think of Klout like a popularity contest or a list a middleschool student might keep to measure the cool factor of other students. Klout did not return press inquiries for this book, and the com-

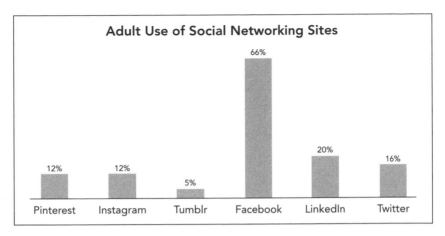

Figure 2.2   "Statistics reveal that 46 percent of Internet users post original photos and videos online they have created themselves and that 41 percent curate photos and videos they find elsewhere on the Internet and post on image-sharing sites. Women are more likely than men to use Pinterest, whereas Instagram and Tumblr attract equal shares of men and women."
Source: The Pew Internet & American Life Project: Photos and Videos as Social Currency, August 2012.

pany has since changed the description of what it does on its website. But as recently as fall of 2012, its website stated that it measured online influence by taking information from across a person's social networks, such as likes, posts, retweets, and photos, and using it to extrapolate an individual's influence.[29] The company's theory, which has been widely criticized, was that influence is determined by how many people an individual engages on social media across the web. It now states that "Klout began with a very simple idea: Everyone has influence—the ability to drive action. Klout built on this idea to show anyone how he or she can influence the world and its future." Klout, founded in 2009 by Joe Fernandez, uses social media activity to provide you a Klout Score. That score measures your influence.

Now, some say they are unsure whether Klout or the many social influence websites like it (Kred or Peerindex) are truly able to measure influence.

"I don't see what value they have, honestly. Influence changes on a dime in the world of social media," Matthew Yeomans, co-author of the book *#Fail: The 50 Greatest Social Media Screw-Ups and How to Avoid Being the Next One*, told me during an interview via Skype from his home in London. Look at it this way: "I could be really influential to one person and not influential at all to another," Yeomans said. "What everyone is trying to do is get algorithms to analyze conversations and people," he added. "Would I make a decision about hiring someone based on their Klout score? If I did I don't think I'd be a very good recruiter."

Perhaps what is more important is to realize that people are beginning to scrutinize a person's connections.

Recruiters, for example, have always checked a person's references. With LinkedIn, recruiters are not only looking at individual profiles, but they can look at a person's connections on the site or other social networking sites and try to extrapolate whether that person may know someone who might be a good fit for their companies.

As SHRM's Curtis Midkiff and I point out during our social media presentations for HR professionals, people are not beholden to traditional organizational charts anymore. Influencers are no longer solely those at the top: boards of directors, CEOs, vice presidents, division heads, team leads, etc. The influencers today might be those who possess information (like the receptionist at work who speaks to everyone entering the building). These are people who are easily accessible—especially if they are using social media to be heard.

Social media is growing at an accelerated speed, and this is only the beginning. Even as you hold this book in your hand, someone somewhere is coming up with another social networking site that may enhance or eclipse what is presently out there—and more sites are being created and expanding daily.

BEST PRACTICES FOR SOCIAL MEDIA
USE @ WORK: ADVICE FOR MANAGERS

- Familiarize yourself with the social media networks your employees are using. Is it Facebook? Instagram? Viddy? Snapchat? Pinterest? Twitter? GetGlue? LinkedIn? Yammer? Don't know? Ask them!
- Do not discourage your employees from using social media. Not only does it hinder engagement, collaboration, innovation, and knowledge sharing; it breeds resentment and mistrust among your most valuable assets—your employees.

- Recognize that even if your company has no social media presence, your employees' use of these tools may be creating one.
- More people visit Facebook than any other site online. It is how we get our news, communicate with our families, and stay abreast of current events and trends. Stop blocking employees from Facebook. It is pointless. They are accessing it on their smartphones under their desks anyway. Give employees guidance, and treat them like responsible adults who do the jobs you hire them to do.
- Remind employees nothing they delete from a social networking site ever really disappears. It lives on the site's servers and can be subpoenaed if necessary—just like people.
- Encourage employees to use social media appropriately in the workplace—create and update LinkedIn, Twitter, or SHRM Connect profiles. Use Foursquare to check in to work or Yammer or other enterprise social media platforms for engagement in and out of the office. But give employees guidelines for appropriate use and behavior. Remind them to think twice about what they post because photos, updates, and links that could be misconstrued or damaging to their company's reputation could lead to their dismissal—if not part of protected concerted activity.
- Be mindful of friending subordinates and colleagues on social networking sites—especially if you are managing their performance. Remember: People use Facebook in different ways and for different reasons. Some people adjust privacy settings regularly. Others do not. As an employer, you may encounter things you are not legally supposed to see. We will address that topic later in subsequent chapters.

> *"You cannot find peace by avoiding life."*
>
> —credited to Virginia Woolf

3 | Reconsidering Your Expectations, or All Work and No Play Makes Jack and Jill Dull Employees

WHAT IS THE INTERNET?

"What is the Internet anyway?," Bryant Gumbel asked Katie Couric and another woman in 1994.

One of the women responded, "Internet is that massive computer network that's becoming really big now."

"What? Do you write to it, like mail?" Gumbel asked. Couric was not really sure, so she asked someone off-camera to explain it.

You can see this exchange on YouTube.

It seems odd, even crazy now, but there was a time when employers were afraid to let their employees have Internet access at work. Now we cannot live without it. In time, we will find that we cannot live without social media. It is firmly embedded in our lives. Internet access at work is as essential as having the lights on. So is social media.

FROM ARPANET TO INTERNET: A HISTORY LESSON

Let's pause for a moment in our discussion about social media engagement and take a quick stroll back in time. Did you know that interactive computing and high-speed networks date as far back as the mid-1960s? That was when universities in the United States and some labs first began using this new thing on computers to talk to each other. They called it "electronic mail," and it was the providence of the U.S. Department of Defense's Advanced Research Projects Agency, what would eventually come to be known as the ARPANET, to be the progenitor of what would eventually become a new worldwide mode in communication.

Fast Fact: Johannes Gutenberg created the first mechanized printing press in Europe in the 15th century. In 1876 Alexander Graham Bell patented the telephone, and 128 years later in 2004, Mark Zuckerberg created Facebook. Each man forever revolutionized communication.

Now, let's fast-forward to the early 1990s when people worldwide were beginning to "surf" the web for information. From America Online to Yahoo from Google to Facebook, technological advances have continued to stun corporate America, and human resources has lead the way to managing employees using these cool, new communication tools.

But managing employees was not always easy.

Each new technology has always been greeted with anxiety and apprehension. But employers need to release their fears, trust their employees, and embrace change, especially given that some researchers believe transparency, connectedness, and sharing help build relationships—relationships that can prove beneficial in myriad ways.

"Every new technology that has come into the workplace has been greeted with fear and trepidation—especially by HR," Bill Kutik told me during an interview for this book. Kutik is a technology columnist for *Human Resource Executive* and HREonline and is co-chairman and founder of the HR Technology Conference & Exposition and host of *The Bill Kutik Radio Show*.

"When telephones first came into corporations only the most senior executives were allowed to have them because the fear was lesser employees would waste time with them or get into mischief," Kutik recalled.

"When e-mail first came into the corporation, HR was petrified that a lower level employee would write something inappropriate to a senior executive, not realizing at the time, of course, that the senior executive would never touch a keyboard himself and that his secretary would printout all of his e-mails, he would write his responses on them, and then the secretary would keyboard them back to the person who sent it, so there was really no danger," he said.

And when the World Wide Web put well, the world, at employees' fingertips, corporations were slow to allow access.

I had just joined the Associated Press (AP) when the web was born; typically only one computer in the newsroom had an Internet connection because only one person could access it at a time. E-mail was relatively new, too. I was among a team of AP reporters sent to Penn State University's main campus in College Park, Pennsylvania, to take a course that would show us how to use the Internet and how to use it for research purposes.

Yes, I took a course on how to use the Internet. You can stop laughing now.

Gradually, corporations began to realize that Internet access was not just a privilege, reserved for a select few, but a valuable tool in getting work done.

In 2000 the Pew Internet & American Life Project reported that "38 million full-time workers in the nation have Internet access at their jobs and two-thirds of them (67 percent) go online at least once per day. When they are online, most are doing job-related research and using e-mail."[1] The Internet has also improved their ability to do their jobs.

By 2008, the last year Pew updated those numbers, 62 percent of employed adults said they used the Internet or e-mail at work, saying that although the tools created stress and new demands, the connectivity and flexibility were beneficial.[2]

What's more, according to Pew, in 2012, 69 percent of adult Internet users used social networking sites like Twitter, Facebook, LinkedIn, or Google + .[3]

Today's web aficionado uses social media sites to engage others to make sense of and discuss information. You do not know what you do not know—until you go online to discover what that is *and* discuss it with others. We live in an age of lightning-speed enlightenment. No longer are we just consuming information. We are learning from that information in a fraction of the time it formerly took us, and we are imparting that knowledge to others—whether for work, school or play. The Internet is a means to an end—not just to find information, but to analyze it, discuss it, and extract meaning. Online content is ingested, analyzed, dissected, and disseminated among internal or external communities built by the end user. Web use can make employees work smarter. Engaging with others through social media helps facilitate that.

Studies show that worldwide, leaders are realizing that to remain competitive they need to foster a culture of employee engagement—something social media does.

According to *Creating People Advantage 2012: Mastering HR Challenges in a Two-Speed World*, "HR departments have made modest progress with Web 2.0 tools in their efforts to source and retain people. But they can, and should do much more. Social media and other Web2.0 tools are valuable places for people to discover new career opportunities (both internally and externally), learn about companies, and exchange information and intelligence about which companies are the best to work for."[4]

The report, released by the World Federation of People Management Associations, and the Boston Consulting Group in 2012, also revealed that among the most pressing and vital challenges companies face is developing a leadership model that allows them to adjust to the ways businesses are operating today—that includes adapting and using technology to plan for and manage continuous change (see Table 3.1).

Another critical challenge? Establishing an environment that nurtures employee engagement and that promotes innovation, collaboration and stronger performance. As we have seen, social media can do that, too.

Table 3.1   Topics that Remain of Low Importance to Human Resources

Ranking of importance	Topics with the lowest current capabilities	Topics of lowest future importance	Topics of lowest current importance
#22	Actively using Web 2.0 For HR	Providing shared services and outsourcing human resources	Actively using Web 2.0 for human resources
#21	Integrating global people management and expansion	Integrating global people management and expansion	Providing shared services and outsourcing human resources
#20	Providing shared services and outsourcing human resources	Actively using Web 2.0 for human resources	Integrating global people management and expansion
#19	Managing an aging workforce	Managing an aging workforce	Managing an aging workforce
#18	Managing work/life balance	Managing diversity and inclusion	Managing diversity and inclusion

Source: "Creating People Advantage 2012/Web Survey and analysis. The Boston Consulting group; The World Federation of People Management Associations, 2012.

Experts like Marcia O'Conner say HR professionals should present the risk "side by side with the rewards" of becoming a social business and stress that social media engagement is not only how talent is discovered but how it allows us how to "work together to find the people that we need." She made this comment during the *Human Resource Executive* 15th Annual HR Technology Conference & Exposition, which I attended in Chicago in 2012.

Those people are not just potential candidates—candidates who are desperately needed in an age of severe talent shortages—but experts who can shape and influence work culture.

O'Conner, an HR industry analyst and an expert on collaborative business culture, said HR professionals struggling with leadership buy-in should use analytics to build the business case for using social media. Metrics that matter are more than how many followers a company has or how many likes a posts receives.

For Jay Kuhns, vice president of Human Resources at All Children's Hospital and Health System, Johns Hopkins Medicine, in St. Petersburg, Florida, it boils down to exposure. He told me that he's discovered that the broader the exposure, the better his candidate pool.

"We do a lot of targeting," he said during an interview for this book. On Facebook, "we are able to track where those likes are coming from and the top eight or 10 areas are in cities where there is a free-standing children's hospital," places from which to draw future talent.

He said more than 1,000 applicants apply to the hospital monthly. Not only are they tracking their applicants' physical locations but also whether they are accessing the hospital's website from a desktop or mobile device—which many people are doing with increasing frequency. "That means we have to be mobile-friendly from a Facebook standpoint."

Consider this: "We rebuild hearts on neonatal kids. That's sophisticated work." So when it comes to the hospital's website and its social media presence, Kuhns said, its web presence should be equally as awesome as what they do for infants.

"I'm not interested in how many people are applying for jobs," he added. "What I'm interested in is building relationships with people so they can get to know us and we can get to know them better and as those relationships begin to develop over time," increase the quality of the hospital's talent pool.

All of their online social interactions would not be possible if hospital administrators were blocking his team from using social media.

Remember, successful companies trust their employees to manage their time and to get their work done, and they genuinely want their employees to be connected and engaged.

Just as we have graduated from the use of mainframe computers to the personal ones we hold in the palms of our hands, it is time for us to embrace social media for employee engagement.

ALL ABOARD! SOCIAL MEDIA REALITY CHECK

- Social media is here to stay. It is not a fad or a trend. There may never come a time when you will hear people say, "Remember that social media thing?"

- It might one day replace snail mail, e-mail, or a ringing telephone. Its importance will only continue to grow and change.
- Should you use it? Your organization needs to consider using social media and to decide if it can enrich your firm's brand, grow the bottom line, and improve organizational goals. So, yes, you probably should.
- Strategy is imperative and having one that applies to the entire company is critical. Once developed and put in place, the strategy will ensure that the commitment, energy, and time invested in social media activities have been worth it.
- Be there. You cannot erect social media accounts and then ignore the audience there. Just as plants need water and sunlight to survive, social media audiences need engagement, feedback, and attention. Do not just broadcast your message. Listen, engage, share, and be reciprocal.
- To use social media is to be engaged. Social media is about sharing, innovating, and collaborating. Be attentive. Be honest. Be transparent and apologetic when necessary, provide feedback whenever possible, and most of all again, be present. Investing the energy, talent, and resources required to maintain your corporate presence within the social media sites you choose to inhabit will be beneficial over time.

> *"Every generation needs a new revolution."*
>
> —Thomas Jefferson

4 | Why Social Media Engagement Is Important, or Why Facebook and Twitter, and LinkedIn Are Not Evil

Newsflash, employers: Employees are going to use Facebook, LinkedIn, and Twitter at work.

You should let them.

Studies show that e-mail is rapidly becoming a dying communication tool. Many firms have turned to using a combination of the telephone, instant messaging, and creating their own social networking sites—not just so their workers can communicate with friends, but with colleagues, experts, and others to help them in their jobs.

Progressive HR professionals are also harnessing the power of social networking tools to nurture, retain, and engage talent and staff. Employers should treat it as they would any other tool, but it should be customized to the organization's culture and its people strategy.

As we saw in the previous chapter, All Children's Health System in Florida has taken that approach.

"We've completely integrated social media into how we practice HR now," Jay Kuhns, SPHR, the hospital's vice president of HR and author of the *No Excuses* blog told me in an interview for this book.

But it was not easy. Kuhns began his social media use like most people—hesitantly. Then, as he began to grow more comfortable and to build his network, he told me he encouraged his staff of 25 to do the same.

"I said we are going to try a bunch of things; some are going to work," he recalled. "If things don't work, don't waste your time doing them anymore and so that alleviated some of the anxiety about trying things we'd never tried before."

It is a strategy that has many in human resources sitting up and taking notice.

"Part of the social push is an outgrowth of our transformation this past year," he said in an interview for this book in October 2012. "So we have a separate and distinct HR Facebook page—separate from the hospital. We have a separate and distinct Twitter account, which is branded with the same name . . . as the Facebook page. We have a careers page on LinkedIn. We have a Pinterest account, and the hospital has a fairly robust YouTube channel. We have the five major social media channels right at the top of the website." And although all of the hospital's recruiters have bios and contact information online, Kuhns' staff does not use the platforms to blast out job openings. They are using them to engage potential employees, connect with the community, and inform customers, clients, anyone, really, on pediatric medicine, health and wellness, and what it is like to live and work in the St. Pete community.

In fall of 2012, the hospital launched a talent community for registered nurses. One of the new nurses in its critical care residency program was preparing to start a blog where she would "share her daily experiences as a brand new nurse." So people could get a window into, "what's scary, what's exhilarating, what's frustrating," Kuhns said. She will be "keeping it very real and putting it out there for people to see and learn and follow. For her personally, it helps her build her brand as a new young professional. For us it's another differentiator, of which we have many here, that separates us from other health care employers—not only in Florida, but nationally, because we recruit nationally every day."

Kuhns does not restrict his staff from engaging in social media. "We felt like we were early adopters for the industry in our area," he said. "It was an exciting thing for us. We read about our industry, share content, [and] participate in Twitter chats, and we started to create this energy." As for his employees, "I want them to spend time on social media. I want them to build their personal brands, because that all comes back to help us."

Kuhns said he embraces social media in a transparent way, blending himself across multiple social media channels. Everyone is not comfortable in sharing in that way, and they do not have to be. But many people are finding that turning to their social networks broadens their abilities to collaborate and innovate as well as gain information, find solutions to problems, and get solid advice—often at lightening speeds.

"It has helped me—the positives have so far outweighed the negatives," Kuhns said. "The resources that are available—it's just mind boggling how much content there is to pull from . . . particularly in an HR role."

SOCIAL CROWD SOURCING CAN ENHANCE PERFORMANCE

What is social crowdsourcing?

Well, it is brainstorming on social networking sites. Think of it as Wikipedia-lite. It is creating your own community of practice among your followers or peers—solely to garner ideas, to innovate, and to gain fresh perspectives. As James Surowiecki pointed out in his book, *The Wisdom of Crowds*, "Under the right circumstances, groups are remarkably intelligent, and are often smarter than the smartest people in them."[1] Therefore, turning to "collective intelligence" of each other— friends, peers, colleagues, and experts—can help people in their jobs.

Where can workers find the biggest crowds? On social networking sites.

According to a July 2012 report from the McKinsey Global Institute, 1.5 billion people are now using social networking sites worldwide to seek the wisdom of their friends.[2] Knowledge workers spend 28 hours every week not just writing e-mails but conducting research and using social media to solve problems and work on tasks with colleagues worldwide.. The report states, too, that "hundreds of millions of people have adopted new behaviors using social media—conducting social activities on the Internet, creating and joining virtual communities, organizing political activities." As the report so astutely puts it, "All the rituals and rites in which individuals and groups in society participate—from personal events such as weddings or daily gossip, to global happenings such as the Arab Spring—play out on social platforms. Indeed, many behaviors that sociologists study—forming, maintaining, and breaking social bonds—are now taking place online."

Social media allows people to engage with one another, whether near or far, in ways that have never been done before—through conversation on websites and in mobile apps, links to articles and videos, graphics, charts, research, music, games, films, and other content housed online. It is actually enhancing our interactions. Today, social media engagement has made the world smaller by bringing the collective knowledge of policy-makers, influencers, and regular Joes and Janes into one space—the Internet—and in most cases, in the palm of a hand. Communication is not limited to the modern-day equivalent of the pony express—newspapers, the telephone, or e-mail on computers, either. This is not just social business; *it is social strategy*. This way of communicating is transformative, and because the nature of this instantaneous communication has the tendency to spread in ways that can and often do come back to haunt us, that fear alone prompts many employers to want to outlaw, curtail, or restrict this way of interacting. No longer are people getting news about such current events as the election or weather emergencies from newspaper sites or television. Increasingly, they are having news sites feed into their social media streams, turning to their friends on Facebook, or seeing what is trending on Twitter to analyze and make sense of that and other information in the world around them.

"In 2008, Symantec partnered with Globoforce, which provides social recognition solutions, to create a single, global employee recognition program called Applause," according to a white paper published by Globoforce.[3]

Applause looks like a social network where employees can congratulate subordinates and each other by spreading "goodwill across the company, helping unify the workforce behind a shared culture and purpose." Not only has the program strengthened employee engagement, Symantec has been able to use the data harnessed to identify and laud top performers as well as, "monitor individual and departmental interaction, and use peer-to-peer recognition data to provide a new viewpoint into employee performance," the white paper states.

"As an HR leader, I now have actionable data. I can show leaders exactly what is happening around rewards, and recognition in their business units," Tom Aurelio, Symantec's vice president of global human resources stated in the paper. "Now as leaders, we can sit down and figure out who . . . our influencers are throughout the business, using the information that comes from Globoforce," he stated.[4]

Something else to consider: "We've seen almost a tectonic change in the workplace around the expectations of workplace culture—a lot of that has been fueled by social media," said Geoff Webb, Aon Hewitt's senior sourcing specialist for LexisNexis in Canada and founder and former CEO of SocialHR, in an interview for this book. "Social media has democratized information," Webb told me. Ten years ago, prospective employees read up on a company by perusing the company brochure or visiting its website. "Now I can go on Google, Facebook, Twitter, Pinterest—there are so many places [where] I can find information." Including Glassdoor, where employees rate employers. Even if a company is not trying to be transparent, "you are transparent because your employees are putting information out there," Webb pointed out.

Don't believe him? Google your firm, or turn to socialmention.com or kurrently.com, search engines that scroll through conversations posted on public social networking sites to see what comes up.

Unlike newspapers, social media is not for captive audiences. It is for participators—those who are hungry for information and are willing to discuss it as they share what they know with others in their networks.

A 2012 United Kingdom study revealed that the average Briton spent 7.5 hours a week on social networking sites between the hours of 9 to 5.[5] Moreover, the respondents admitted they spent more time on those sites at work than they did at home. Employers may not like employees using these sites to communicate with not just their friends but with each other about working conditions, but there is no escaping it—especially now. In 2012 the NLRB ruled that workers can legally discuss their working conditions on social networking sites.[6] It is called protected concerted activity.

Employers must realize that the ways in which employees communicated (and found jobs) in the past are basically a thing of the past. According to Cisco's *2012 Connected World Technology Report*, 91 percent of college students use Facebook, and 81 percent of those students check their accounts every day. The report revealed that "90 percent of Gen Y surveyed worldwide said they check their smartphones for updates in e-mail, texts and social media sites, often before they get out of bed."[7] Employees in 2013 and beyond will expect to use Facebook, LinkedIn, and Twitter—even at work. And in the war for talent—good talent—employers must choose between allowing their employees to use such sites or face the realization that when people are forced to choose between being able to use such tools in the workplace, experts say, they will choose the tools over the job.

"We the older generation—the Baby Boomers—have got to understand that these Millennials—who are going to be inheriting our jobs in a few years—do things differently from the way we do them," John Greer, senior consultant at JA Greer Associates told me when I interviewed him for *SHRM Online* in an interview in 2008.[8]

Social media use has not really been limited to young people.

He declined to be interviewed for the book shortly after he spoke at the Social Media and Advocacy Summit sponsored by the Public Affairs Council in Washington, D.C., on July 24, 2012, but, from the stage, George Alafoginis, who oversees client partnerships for Facebook's politics and government division said, "We are no longer the college-aged based website. Most of our users are between 45 and 55."

He Posted What? A Social Case Study

Employees should also be made aware of their company's confidentiality policies so corporate secrets or customer information is not divulged online, as was in the case of an employee who worked at ACE Cash Express.

"We had an employee who decided to use Facebook to talk about a customer who had come in and cashed a large check—and made light of how much [the customer] cashed it for," Elizabeth Lalli-Reese, SPHR, an HR consultant in Irving, Texas, said in an interview for this book. ACE is a check-cashing establishment with 1,800 retail locations in 35 states and the District of Columbia.

A former employment and labor attorney, Lalli-Reese said the employee disclosed the store's location and described the person who cashed the check, which was worth thousands of dollars.

"A fellow employee sent us screen shots," of the interaction, she said, and human resources could see that "people responded to the post [with] things like 'I could have stopped him at the door.' Well, that's a huge liability, because it's out there for the public to see," Lalli-Reese said. Anyone with malicious intent had the store's location and a description of the customer, putting both employees and customers in danger.

Because the action did not "seem malicious" the employee was not fired, she said.

"At the time we didn't have a social media policy in place—so it was more of an opportunity to educate that employee as well as the staff about the proper social media etiquette," Lalli-Reese continued. Up until that time, a social media policy "wasn't something we had really thought about in-depth and so we didn't really want to crack the whip on what we thought was probably an innocent mistake," she said. "It was a teachable moment—and really we felt like we had failed to inform, educate, and have a policy in place."

• •

Many employers are afraid that employees will limit their social media use to wasting time on Facebook or that they will blab company secrets on Twitter. However, these issues can be mitigated by establishing policies governing social media use at work and by training employees on those policies. Chapter 9 outlines how to do just that.

Do not just construct policies, added Craig Fisher, vice president of LinkedIn training, social media strategy, and workforce marketing for Ajax Social Media. "People should absolutely be trained on it [and] it needs to reflect how employees interact with the outside world. Most people don't know the employee handbook . . . and still do whatever they want online. You can be as strict as you want, but [not having a policy is] like putting your head in the sand and pretending like it's not there. You need to educate people on it," he told me during an interview for this book.

Especially given that social media use is growing.

For many, social networking has become as ubiquitous as e-mail, as necessary as the telephone. "If your boss told you you're not allowed to call your wife from the office, I think people would view that as being unnecessarily draconian," Nick Stein, director of content and media at Rypple.com, told *SHRM Online* in an interview in June 2012. "Facebook has, in many ways, become the new phone. It's, in many cases, a better way for people to communicate, whether it's for business or non-business purposes."[9]

But if companies continue to block employees from these sites, Stein said, how are they "going to view an organization that is policing their ability to be who they are?"

Younger employees are already at the forefront of this transformation.

At the end of 2011, Bersin & Associates listed more than a dozen predictions for HR professionals in 2012, including a need for human resources to "drive engagement programs for workers who are under the age of 30."[10] This prediction is especially relevant because experts predict that by the year 2020, Millennials will make up close to half of the workforce.

Part of that need for engagement must include the use of social media tools and the ability of people to access them. Yet according to SHRM research from 2011, some organizations block employee access to such social networking sites, including YouTube, the world's second-largest search engine.[11] Employers also blocked employees from photo-sharing applications fearing, most likely, that employees would waste time on them. But employees will find ways around blocked sites on company devices. At least one study showed more people were accessing such sites while at work because their smartphones allowed them to do so more discreetly. According to a 2013 study by IDC and Facebook, two of the most popular activities on a smartphone were viewing and responding to e-mail (78 percent) and checking Facebook (70 percent); in fact, people check Facebook on average 14 times per day.[12] Facebook's Alafoginis said in summer of 2012 at the aforementioned conference where I was in the audience that of the site's active users in the United States, 70 percent return daily, and 111 million access the site through their smartphones monthly.

According to the IDC and Facebook study, 67.8 percent of the population in the United States will use smartphones by 2017. Perhaps what's even more telling is that 40 percent of those surveyed said they feel "connected" when using Facebook to send messages; 49 percent when they send text messages and 43 percent when they talk on the phone. "People have a universal need to connect with others, especially those they care deeply about. This coupled with mass market adoption of smartphones means that social engagement via phones has become mainstream." The study also revealed that not only are 70 percent of people accessing Facebook from a smart device, but, between Monday and Sunday, "84 percent of respondents' time is spent on phone communicating via text, e-mail, and social media versus only 16 percent on phone calls." That's right. More people are typing than talking.[13]

But even with all this use, experts say the rewards of employee engagement may outweigh the perceived loss of productivity. "Internal social media is an untapped resource for recruitment and retention," Scott Healy, who conducted research on the topic for Gagen MacDonald said during an interview for this book.

"Plenty of companies are using LinkedIn and other tools [to recruit] but internally, the more you use internal social media, the more you help your HR function" by improving employee engagement, Healy said.

But still, "I understand the hesitation to want to block it," Jessica Lee, SPHR, director of digital talent strategy for Marriott International, added during a phone interview. "But if you're not making it accessible, people are going to find ways around it. They're going to use their phones or find other ways to be unproductive . . . people are going to be unproductive with or without social media."

Jessica Miller-Merrell, SPHR, author of *Tweet This! Twitter for Business*, said HR needs to be aware that "there's workarounds," such as website proxies. "An employee can pay $9.99 a month that allows them to bypass the servers and search on the company's Internet. For IT, it looks like they're on one website, but in reality they're surfing the web unrestricted and . . . nobody knows what they're doing."

Interviewed while attending SHRM's Talent Management Conference in 2012, Miller-Merrell said she once worked at a company that expected her to be there "65 hours a week. How could I be there and not check Wikipedia, or the bank, or other sites? Complete restrictions lead people to do this," she said, holding up an iPhone.

"People are bringing in their own devices, and the VPs of HR are doing it, too," she added. Some work computers are so restricted that "some people can't read blogs, can't check the local weather. If you don't trust your people they're not going to reciprocate and trust you back. They're not going to do their best work because they'll feel like they're in jail. It leads to a toxic culture and high turnover in your organization," she said. Though visiting social networking sites does have its risks—risk of loss of employee productivity, potential loss of intellectual property, and IT security concerns, "it does allow employees to garner information and conduct research," Miller-Merrell said.

The Pew Internet & American Life Project reported in early 2012 that one in five adults in the United States does not use the Internet.[14] Those include some Spanish-speaking respondents, those without a high-school education, and those "living in households earning less than $30,000 per year who are least likely to have Internet access." Pew reports that 58 percent of all adults who do use the Internet have researched a product or service online. Studies show that when people are stumped for answers, they often turn to crowdsourcing— turning to their friends, peers, or networks to seek information or advice or to solve a problem. They engage people on social networking sites[15] in search of advice.[16] SHRM sees it every day in the web traffic on HR Talk. HR professionals have been going to HR Talk since 2001—just to seek advice from other HR professionals. The statistics show that HR Talk has major web traffic, consisting mostly of HR professionals working collaboratively. Studies show employees do not work through their organizational charts anymore to find answers to questions, SHRM's Anne-Margaret Olsson told me during an interview. Olsson manages the social networking and online communities for SHRM. They pose those questions to their social networks. They reach out first to people they know for answers, Olsson added.

Miller-Merrell concurred.

"I use my Twitter like a Google search engine in real time," Miller-Merrell said. "Within five minutes, I can get information. I don't have to read a white paper. People are telling me right away. Even Quora is more academic." She said HR professionals and managers should realize that "people want to be entertained as well as educated and that's why social networking sites are popular. It's kind of like going to the golf course—you're talking business, but you're also playing," she told me during our interview shortly after we helped lead a presentation on social media use at a SHRM conference in 2012.

Social media has forever changed the ways in which office workers work. Companies need to realize that just because employees are at work behind a firewall, their communication habits outside of work are not going to change.

"Why would we neglect the fact that people now have shifted in how they interact with each other both professionally and personally and limit the tools at their disposal behind the firewall?" asks Healy. "There's just too much evidence that this is how we communicate," he told me.

FORGET CONTROL; ADOPT INTEGRATION

Instead of trying to control social media use, experts say, employers should integrate these new tools to expand and deepen their employees' knowledge as well as improve business strategy. By fall of 2012, many software vendors were offering social business platforms that could be integrated into customer relationship management (CRM) or enterprise resource planning ERP) systems and applicant tracking systems (ATS). Adoption is easier if social tools are integrated within existing business applications already in place. That integration allows for collaborative applications like instant messaging, audio and video conferencing, the ability to share and work together on documents, and e-mail, as well as social networks such as YouTube, Facebook, Twitter, and LinkedIn.

You can see an example of this by watching PepsiCo's Gatorade Mission Control YouTube video. PepsiCo uses social media to monitor what people are saying about its Gatorade brand.[17]

Companies are discovering that by allowing their employees to network with each other and with people outside of work, they are able to solve challenges, obtain information, and help customers, as well as grow their brands.

This kind of collaboration can work. But first culture has to change. Expectations have to change, but a social media strategy is imperative first. Many organizations jump into social media without realizing the return on investment because they did not strategize first. As SHRM's research points out, more than one-quarter (28 percent) of organizations have a social media strategy. Larger organizations were more likely to have a social media strategy than smaller firms, and those with U.S.-based operations were more likely to have one than those based outside the United States.

Implementing a social media strategy will, in effect, lead to constructive, vibrant relationships with workers and their leaders and may improve essential business operations, eliminate silos, and foster a work environment where employees feel trusted to use social networking to engage and collaborate not just with their friends but with their peers and colleagues as well. The strategy should help employers properly create, manage, and measure effective workplace policies, too.

But the first step is to make sure business leaders and HR professionals are well informed about social media use and how it can benefit a company in the long run—not just through recruitment efforts but through employee engagement as well.

"HR people in general need to have an understanding of how these tools are being used," Miller-Merrell said, during our interview. "I don't think they have a choice anymore."

Fear of unproductive employees may not be the reality.

For example, there are numerous platforms that interact with social media sites, and Facebook and Twitter messages and blog posts can be scheduled. Just because something is time-stamped at 10 a.m. when an employee was in a meeting does not mean it was actually posted at that time. Managers need to understand how social media and social media platforms operate.

After all, "if HR people don't understand social media, how are we going to expect our employees" to understand social media? Miller-Merrell said.

Social media advocate Lars Schmidt, who is senior director of talent acquisition and innovation at National Public Radio (NPR), said in a phone interview that he has three dozen websites aggregating content into Google Reader.

"I work for a nonprofit," Schmidt said. "I'm doing a lot of hands on recruiting myself and there are a lot of things I'm responsible for, so I realized early on that I'm hyper efficient with my time on social media."

In addition to Google Reader, for example, "once or twice a week on my commute I'll scour all of the latest articles and if they are articles that I think are relevant to my communities, I will flag it, and I use a tool called Buffer to schedule those posts."

This, Schmidt said, helps him makes effective use of his time on social media.

5 | Embracing Social Media

As we have seen, ignoring the seamless way social media exists in our lives is like trying to find a light switch on the ceiling in the dark. Managers who block their employees from visiting social sites are like drivers who suddenly slam on the brakes when everyone behind them is driving 80 miles an hour. Social networking and its use is continuing to grow, and at a faster rate than any other medium in history.

Whether you are managing employees who use social media or diving into it for the first time for personal or professional reasons, not only should you be aware of how social media works, but you need to know that embracing social media communications internally and externally is a necessity for growing the business.

Companies are now using social media to share content, improve brand awareness, increase traffic to their websites, engage with customers and colleagues, grow their marketing contacts while decreasing their marketing expenses, improve their companies' reputations, address problems and provide solutions as well as provide feedback to clients and customers as well as employees, increase the quantity and quality of business leads, improve customer service and search engine rankings, and increase revenue as well, SHRM research revealed.[1]

What's more, companies like GE, Marsh & McLennan Companies, Deloitte, IBM, and many others are mimicking the culture of Facebook engagement with their own private, internal social networks to retain data and to help employees collaborate and work more efficiently. Many, like IBM, have built platforms that do just that for other companies, too. And although these social business tools often mirror ones used outside the enterprise, they are built specifically to serve business needs and are more secure.

"We're certainly finding that the next generation workforce expects employees to share, post, update, and communicate with their colleagues and customers using social networking tools to get real work done," Sandy Carter, vice president, social business sales and evangelism at IBM stated in an e-mail interview conducted for this book. "This is a fact and organizations are quickly learning that being social isn't just about having a Facebook page and a Twitter account. A social business means that every department in the organization has embedded social capabilities into their traditional business processes to fundamentally impact how work gets done to create business value. A social business utilizes social software technology to communicate with its rich ecosystem of clients, business partners and employees. IBM has been practicing this for years and is seeing real business value because of it."

For example, "as one of the largest consumers of social technologies, IBM is a case study for the transformation into a social business," Carter continued. "This goes beyond IBM's business in social software and services," which also provides collaboration software, consulting services, analytics, social media research, and conducting brainstorming sessions for clients.

IBM leads social business in technology, policy, and practice.

Carter said companies should consider IBM's history in social media:

- For 15 years, long before Millennials became fixated with social networking sites like Myspace and Facebook, IBM employees were using social software to foster collaboration among a dispersed 400,000-person team, Carter said.
- In 1997, at a time when many companies were seeking to restrict their employees' Internet use, IBM recommended that its employees go online, Carter added.
- In 2005 the company made a strategic decision to embrace blogging and encouraged its staff to do so as well.
- In 2007 IBM launched Connections, its own social networking software for the enterprise.
- In early 2008, IBM introduced social computing guidelines that included sharing media and the use of virtual worlds like Second Life. Later that year, IBM opened its Center for Social Software to help the company's global network of researchers collaborate with corporate residents, university students, and faculty, creating what many consider the industry's premier incubator for the research, development, and testing of social software that is "fit for business," Carter wrote via e-mail
- Today, IBM provides the industry's leading social software platform to clients; International Data Corporation (IDC) has ranked IBM No.1 in worldwide market share for enterprise social software and has since 2010.

Yet, despite the trail that IBM has blazed, convincing companies to embrace the added benefits of this new form of internal communication is admittedly harder—especially if these same firms are blocking employees from communicating with their personal, external social networks.

However, recent trends in internal-communications software demonstrate these companies may soon be the exception, not the rule.

In fact, social media software for the enterprise, like IBM's Connections or Microsoft's Yammer, is one of the most rapidly growing markets in the software industry—now more commonly referred to as social task management or STM. IDC reported in 2012 that adoption for enterprise social software is expected to grow considerably through 2016.[2] IDC expects revenue from such software to grow from $0.8 billion in 2011 to $4.5 billion in 2016.

"It is critical for social software solutions to keep up with the pace of change to meet emerging business needs," Michael Fauscette, group vice president for IDC's software business solutions group, stated in a release on the company's website in June 2012.[3] "IDC expects acquisition activity to continue apace and that social solutions will rapidly evolve and converge around business critical workflow." Not only should vendors embrace these changes; "users should act in anticipation of them," he stated.

These tools work in tandem with common task management software that can improve communication and help employees distribute information, work together, and solve problems rapidly.

Dashboards and activity streams are blended within these social task management tools, and they help workers track projects. By updating their "statuses" in these streams, they can show colleagues all the recent events that have occurred, for example, when new assignments are being made or have been finished, when new pages have been created, or when files have been uploaded, according to *Getting Work Done With Social Task Management*, a 2012 report by Constellation Research.[4]

Encouraging people to change the ways in which they are accustomed to working is difficult. But by blending these tools into a person's daily work habits, companies make it easier for employees to get the information they need more immediately "instead of looking in one place for assignments, another for conversations and another for content," writes Alan Lepofsky, a vice president and principal analyst at Constellation Research.

For example, General Electric (GE) developed its own social networking site called GE Colab. In an interview with the *MIT Sloan Management Review* in November 2012, Ron Utterbeck, CIO for GE's corporate and the Advanced Manufacturing Software Technology Center in Michigan, told the publication that the company's 115,000 employees bring video, e-mail, and chat discussions into its "stream."[5]

"What we wanted to do was bring those together into a platform," he said. As a result, Utterbeck told the publication, "We're solving problems faster. When you belong to these groups and you can see how people are saying, 'Hey, I got this problem,' literally, within minutes, three or four people comment on it and say, 'Have you tried this? What about this?' People are connecting, finding the people they need. Like, 'I need a compliance officer in India. I have this issue that I need to bounce off of somebody.'"

Salesforce has a platform called Do.com, and two Facebook alums, Dustin Moskovitz and Justin Rosenstein, started Asana.[6]

"Instead of a social graph, we want to give you a work graph—a task graph of all the things you're working on or have worked on—where you can see—at a glance—what things you need to accomplish, and the next goal, and the next goal after that—all that management of work driving to the successful completion of projects," former Facebook engineer Rosenstein told *Information Week*.[7]

In 2010, global insurance firm Marsh & McLennan Companies launched Marsh University, a social collaboration platform used by 25,000 employees in more than 100 countries. At an HR technology convention in Chicago that I attended in late 2012, the company's chief human resources officer Laurie Ledford and senior vice president & global director of enterprise communications and colleague engagement Ben Brooks discussed how the insurance firm was able to harness its employees' expertise by encouraging them to teach each other about things both related and unrelated to work.

Contained within the site, which the company refers to as a "university," employees use blogs, videos, and other social media functions to educate and collaborate to better serve its businesses worldwide.

In summer of 2012, IBM purchased social business leader Kenexa—specifically, it said, to accelerate the company's ability to help clients embrace social business capabilities.

"Twofold to creating business value for the organization, we're seeing that social has a direct impact in creating a smarter workforce," Sandy Carter said in an interview for this book. "Using social tools internally and externally, employees can quickly and easily find expertise, share knowledge, and ultimately grow the corporate brain," she said.

Yet despite the innovative uses of social media within the enterprise, some studies show people still fear embracing it—mainly because they are afraid of what employees may do online.

Like the Applebee's waitress who was fired in January 2013 after she reportedly posted a receipt in which a customer had written, "I give God 10%, why should I give you 18?"[8]

Fast Fact: More than 67,000 social business communities have been developed by IBM, and 475,000 files shared globally have generated more than 9 million downloads. Every day, IBM generates 35 million instant message chats, too.

HR experts say the easiest way employers and employees can get over the fear of using these new communication tools is to realize that they are simply tools—and have employees govern their behavior accordingly—*with policies*. After all, companies are not monitoring each and every single e-mail and telephone call before it goes out, are they? Social media tools used outside of the enterprise allow people not only to network but to educate themselves.

SOCIAL MEDIA IS EVOLVING BUSINESS PROCESSES

Marsh & McLennan Companies gave employees a role to play in their social media engagement. They helped colleagues develop relationships not just to foster employee engagement but to tap their collective knowledge across all kinds of topics.

"People want to be recognized," Brooks said at the conference. So the company encouraged employees to use the social networking portal to be "genuine with clients and each other," he said, and to be nimble and flexible and to move quickly to deliver quality results. Employees were encouraged to express their candid points of view and to encourage others to do the same. They were told to have constructive debates—even if they disagreed—and to speak up when they had ideas—even if those ideas challenged the status quo. Employees were asked to be inclusive, to be open to diverse ideas, experiences, and backgrounds, to trust each other, and to act with integrity and to be ethical.

"This is something we're continuing to grow in," Brooks said.

During *Human Resource Executive*'s 15th Annual HR Technology Conference & Exposition, where Marsh & McLennan Companies gave its presentation, dozens of vendors unveiled products embedded with social networking features and technologies—a new trend that is continuing to grow. Today's social media world might be likened to a modern-day equivalent of a community of practice, a group of individuals who come together to learn from one another through regular interactions.

"I've been monitoring this for a while," Yvette Cameron, vice president and principal analyst of HCM Processes at Constellation Research, a San Francisco-based technology research firm, said in an interview for this book. Social media tools "are coming in through corporate IT initiatives; they're coming in through teams. People are really trying to bypass the hierarchy and decision barriers that are in place to get work done and be efficient and get that collaboration and brainstorming going," she noted. The technology is entering the enterprise because people are using it outside the office to get things done, and they expect to be able to use the same kinds of tools inside to do the same. "HR has said 'Oh, it's too scary. It's too risky," Cameron added. "But the reality is that everybody, including HR is recognizing that this isn't a technology that is going to go away."

Much as the Internet is not going anywhere, social media is "really just a manifestation of how we want to work and engage and get access to information and accelerate the knowledge flow so we can move on to the next thing," she said. "Social technologies seem to be the best approach to do that today."

Companies like eBay, Ford, Charles Schwab, T-Mobile, Deloitte, GE, and Marsh & McLennan Companies are just a few firms using social business platforms provided by IBM, Yammer, Accenture, Jive, or Salesforce, or are using platforms they developed on their own—on a number of different scales. Just as they do on Facebook, Twitter, and LinkedIn, people are using these internal platforms to collaborate and learn. They are also taking notes, tracking tasks, using chat rooms and instant messaging, working on projects, organizing meetings and events, and closing deals. Not only are they posting documents, links, photos and videos; revising calendars; and sending reminders, updating the status of projects, Power Points, to-do lists, spreadsheets, files, and other documents—to do real, productive work—they are finding experts within their companies in different divisions in and outside the countries in which the operate and across silos to help them work more efficiently.

"Where [the use] becomes successful is in the activity stream. For example, where I'm not just told, 'Hey I just posted a great document but there's a link to the document or better yet, it's a video . . . where I can actually launch the video in the activity stream,'" Cameron said. "It becomes even more beneficial—and this is where Oracle is going with its solution and where Salesforce is delivering in its application today—is when I am in my business tool, my CRM [customer relationship management] tool and I'm engaging with the customer [and] I can actually collaborate with those in my company around that customer and their issue . . . and have all that collaboration happen in the context of the business application I'm working in already," she said.

But getting people to see the business value in using these tools is part of the battle. Just because no one is commenting on a post does not mean people are not reading it. For example, in winter of 2012, Facebook began to show group and page creators the numbers of people who saw a post, whether in their news feed or ticker, or on their wall or in a page post from a friend. This example reiterates the importance of engagement.

PARTICIPATION EQUALS ENGAGEMENT

So, what is the best way to begin to participate? Lurk! Although this may be an uncomfortable term in the world of human resources, it is not in the realm of social media. With Twitter, for example, "you can create lists and identify and follow the top people in that particular space and watch and observe," said NPR's senior director, talent acquisition & innovation, Lars Schmidt during a phone interview.

"You don't necessarily have to be tweeting yourself to get value from Twitter," he said. "You can sit back and see what the smartest people in your industry are reading, what blogs are inspiring them. What are their reactions to different policy changes and regulations and legal and compliance issues? So somebody who is just a student of their craft has the ability to tap into all of this information in a very efficient and low cost way."

Whereas many companies are using Yammer and Jive and Chatter and their own internal social networks, NPR did something unique.

"I created a private group in Facebook for only NPR employees where people could collaborate and get together and interact," said Schmidt, who also blogs on AmplifyTalent.com. "It's not an official communication channel," he said of the Facebook group, "but I wanted to do something that was organic and easy to use, but not require our employees to develop new behaviors. They know how it works. It was a way for people to have more informal dialogue—and I'm always fascinated by communication and culture and it was an easy, low cost tool to fuel culture and engagement."

NPR uses the group as a "pure collaboration" tool where employees discuss restaurants, flag football games, and use it much like a bulletin board. "The intent was not to be like Microsoft SharePoint's collaboration portal. There aren't any documents," he said. The venture, which he began in mid-August 2012, grew exponentially.

"You have to be a friend to be invited in—I have to cross reference those 'friends' with our personnel files. I sent out the invitations to eight employees I was friends with on Facebook, and they got them to add people. We're a company of 850 and almost 20 percent of our employees signed up within two hours. I was blown away by that, and I thought that it was really cool. Just yesterday someone in our programming group baked a cake with the NPR logo on it. This is more of a cultural communication facilitator that has a positive impact on culture and it's also a behavior you don't need to learn."

People who are members of Facebook groups know, too, that being a member of a group means that group members cannot see each other's pages—unless they are friends or unless those pages are public.

Some companies are not as progressive as NPR. SHRM's research revealed that 39 percent of HR professionals surveyed said their organizations block Facebook; 38 percent block Myspace; 33 percent block Twitter; 32 percent block YouTube; and 16 percent block access to LinkedIn. It is unfortunate that employers fear what they do not understand and that a great many are not allowing access to these channels because they fear failure—especially public failure.

Marketing and advertising guru William Tincup pointed out that companies need to embrace failing and owning up to mistakes because that is where learning begins. He likens it to working out. "When you work out you tear your muscles a little bit and then they repair.

Well that's fear," the CEO of Tincup & Co. told me in a phone interview. "When we make mistakes those are those tiny tears. If there's no tear then there's no growth." There is humility in acknowledging failure. "We love the second chance," Tincup added.

Certainly Red Cross can attest to that. In 2011, a Red Cross employee mistakenly tweeted:

> **American Red Cross**
> @RedCross
>
> Ryan found two more 4 bottle packs of Dogfish Head's Midas Touch beer.... when we drink we do it right #gettngslizzerd
>
> HootSuite · 2/15/11 11:24 PM

The Red Cross acknowledged the mistaken tweet and responded:

> **@RedCross**
> American Red Cross
>
> **We've deleted the rogue tweet but rest assured the Red Cross is sober and we've confiscated the keys.**
>
> 57 minutes ago via ÜberTwitter   ☆ Favorite ⇄ Retweet ↰ Reply
>
> Retweeted by stefsealy and 51 others

Source: Dogfish Head http://redcrosschat.org/2011/02/16/twitter-faux-pas/

Meanwhile, Dogfish Head responded by encouraging its followers to donate to the Red Cross. Every social media mistake does not have to turn into a fiasco.

Be Present

"If you don't have any awareness [of how it works] . . . you become less visible and at a point in the not-to-distant future, you could become a liability," Lars Schmidt of NPR said. "Social media is not a fad," he added. "It's here to stay and it's impacting the world of work—period."

"It's evolving," he said, "and the pace of innovation is accelerating. If people are still skeptical about it, they're going to find themselves outdated pretty quickly."

Fear of the tools or simply ignoring their existence by blocking their use at work is no longer a viable option—in fact research is revealing that not only is collaboration through the use of social media tools the evolution of employee engagement, but that it helps companies manage talent and recruit and retain employees and leads to improvement in productivity.

"The need to engage employees in business to harness collective knowledge and focus on improving business is driving a new generation of technology for social collaboration," said Mark Smith, CEO and chief research officer at Ventana Research.[9] "Companies need to begin moving beyond the use of e-mail and telephone to using Internet based technologies advancing from the methods used in social media and collaboration within the enterprise for human capital management needs."

Strategy execution firm Gagen MacDonald's 2011 Employee Engagement Study analyzed the impact and use of internal social media within corporations.[10] After polling U.S. employees, the company discovered 51 percent of respondents said their firms used internal social media tools, and 61 percent of employees said their companies' social media tools make collaboration easier.

More and more managers and their employers are slowly beginning to realize that using social media—externally and internally—has its benefits.

"Businesses and their leaders are getting over the initial fears about using social tools in the workplace and are recognizing that they

> **Fast Fact:** "More and more companies are adding sites like Yammer and the like and creating their own social networking sites for collaboration and communication—and more importantly, more employees are expecting to use sites like these at work—particularly Gen Y," John Boudreau said. The book further states that "social networks, and in particular, their strategic impact, may be more vital to organizations pursuing strategies that require knowledge, integrating multiple perspectives for sustainability, or spanning organization units to create innovation."
>
> —Edward E. Lawler III and John Boudreau, *Effective Human Resource Management*

have strategic value," Sebastien Marotte, Google's vice president of enterprise for Europe, Middle East, and Africa, stated in Google's 2012 study.[11]

One of the reasons why the enterprise social networking software market is projected to climb is that "research shows that senior managers are recognizing that social tools allow people to transcend business silos, to connect and to share in a way that just wasn't possible before," Marotte remarked.

"In researching my book, I've discovered social media usage is growing—especially at the corporate level," John Boudreau, professor at the University of Southern California (USC), Marshall School of Business, and research director at USC's Center for Effective Organizations, told me during an interview. We were discussing social media and about the new book he co-wrote with Edward E. Lawler, *Effective Human Resource Management*.

Yammer reported in 2013 that more than 80 percent of *Fortune 500* companies are using its services within their enterprises.[12]

It is not alone.

"Deloitte is embedding social media into every aspect of our talent life cycle,"[13] Patricia Romeo, a former HR generalist and leader at Deloitte LLP in Cincinnati, Ohio, said in a session she co-led with human capital and social business consultant Dr. Joseph Press at a conference on work/life flexibility held by SHRM in fall of 2011.

When potential employees interview at Deloitte—where the average employee is 28 years old—they are given links to the profiles of current employees on D Street, Deloitte's internal social network.[14] "This gives potential employees the opportunity to help them connect on different levels—personal levels to help people feel at home when they come to work," she said.

Yammer and D Street, which Deloitte launched in 2008, look a lot like Facebook. Deloitte employees get a personal landing page on D Street, complete with photo gallery, "about me" section, and blog. Their page includes personnel data from the firm's records and other information. D Street has online communities in which employees can engage in conversations or share information about like-minded topics. There, they can collaborate on documents, seek assistance, obtain advice, identify experts, share knowledge, engage in professional development activities, and network.

In a 2011 study by global professional services firm Towers Watson, a majority of companies around the globe said they are becoming more accustomed to using keeping their employees informed through the use of social networking tools.[15] Social media and its inherent way of making people connect on a personal level can help build a bridge to better employee engagement, Dr. Joseph Press added during his discussion with HR professionals at a SHRM conference in 2011.

Gagen MacDonald's Scott Healy agreed.

"There is a direct correlation between internal social media usage and employee engagement," he said during a phone interview for this book. What's the correlation? Retention and recruitment; the perception that a company that uses internal social media is innovative; ease of productivity and collaboration; and "the most striking and the . . . most surprising is that internal social media is positively linked to employee advocacy toward a company above and beyond the call of duty. By that I mean employees are more willing to stick their necks out for a company when social media is being used well internally."

In Gagen MacDonald and APCO Worldwide's joint 2011 online survey of U.S. adults, 58 percent of respondents said they would rather work at a company that utilizes social media tools, and 89 percent said they would recommend their company's products or services to friends and others—if their company was doing a good job with internal social media.[16]

"The workplace is becoming much more open and transparent and much less hierarchical," Rypple.com's Nick Stein said. "The Internet is a metaphor for that. Companies are realizing that in order to compete in today's marketplace, it's no longer possible to do so with a strict hierarchical command-and-control model."[17]

In the Google study, respondents who used social media tools at least once a week, 86 percent said they had been promoted recently and 72 percent believed they would be promoted in the future.[18]

About 71 percent of those in senior management positions said they believed using social networking makes it easier for firms to recruit and keep the best and brightest; 76 percent said they think companies that welcome social networking by their employees would expand faster than those that ignore it. Lastly, 53 percent of senior managers said companies that don't welcome social media with open arms may eventually fail.[19]

Look at it this way: Our society is not just moving toward social media engagement—it is already there. This is our new reality.

"Broadly speaking, what we're seeing is a revolution in the way we connect, communicate, collaborate, and actually organize ourselves to get our work done and that is a transformation that HR should be sitting at the center of and driving," Ryan Estis, chief experience officer for Ryan and Associates told me during an interview for this book. Estis, author of the Passion on Purpose blog, is a leading expert in leadership and culture, sales effectiveness, brand experience, and the future of work.

"You can resist it. You can ignore it. You can wish it wasn't so [but this] is the reality of our new reality and that's where business is going. Like it or not. You can lead change or let change happen to you."

Human resources must lead the charge in embracing social media and educate employees that their behaviors on social networking sites—whether they are physically on the job or not—can damage themselves and their company's reputations. But employers must remember that employees do have the right to discuss their working conditions on these sites, too.

DIVING INTO SOCIAL—
BEST PRACTICES FOR EMBRACING SOCIAL MEDIA

- Consider increasing your knowledge about social media use. Set up a Google alert on social media and read about innovations. New ones occur constantly.
- Afraid to dive in? Visit Twitter, Facebook, Quora, and LinkedIn. Do it today. Set up an account, and watch, read, and listen—before you engage.
- To build or not to build? Be an advocate for starting your firm's internal social network. Yammer and Chatter are some possible platforms. Due diligence can turn the tide toward fostering broader engagement, but that engagement needs to be driven. So plan to have fun and learn while you work. Organize a photo contest or make announcements within the social network. Encourage employees to break silos and collaborate with colleagues, peers, and friends. Do not talk "at people" but listen and contribute value, too.
- Institute a policy on social media engagement. Outline parameters, and decide who the stakeholders will be. HR? Public relations? Marketing? Analyze the use and adoption of your network, and discuss both offline.
- Make the case for external social media engagement in your firm by realizing the strategic value of being in the space inhabited by customers, clients, peers, and colleagues. Recognize, too, that if you are not in the space—your competitors are, leaving your firm at a possible disadvantage.
- Encourage your employees to use social media—responsibly. Be mindful of regulations. Employees are allowed to discuss their jobs on social media. Help them build their brands (while enhancing your firm) through their very own blogs and contributions to Twitter chats, LinkedIn, SHRM Connect groups, and other online forums.

6 | Social Recruiting or Why Job Boards Should Be Afraid of It

There are lots of books on social recruiting, and this chapter is not solely a primer on how to recruit via social networking sites. Rather, it is an explanation of how recruiters are turning to such sites to find people (talent) and why discovering too much information from those social sites could be detrimental for employers.

Recruiters and hiring managers know that, in the race for talent, finding good employees can be hard.

People are not simply snail-mailing letters anymore, and recruiters are not going to career fairs in droves or relying solely on resumes coming into applicant tracking systems, either.

Scores of recruiters now scour LinkedIn, Twitter, Facebook, Google + , Pinterest, and other social networking sites to broaden their applicant pools, find potential hires faster, and save money. In SHRM's survey findings, "Social Networking Websites and Recruiting/Selection," released in spring of 2013, 77 percent of organizations say they use social networking sites to find talent. In 2011, that number stood at 56 percent. It was at 34 percent in 2008.[1] Some companies have crafted branded careers pages on social networking sites and have created career-related Twitter handles from which to broadcast jobs. Many are turning to LinkedIn and other vendors like iCIMS, Kenexa, Oracle, Gild, Jobvite, Jobs2Web, Monster, and a host of others, which have incorporated social media into their recruiting software solutions.

Fast Fact: LinkedIn has more than 200 million members in 200 countries and territories, making it the largest professional network online—and the most lucrative.

Job boards and resume management tools may soon be a relic of the past as recruiters seek to find new employees from what they like to call "passive candidates." These are individuals who are already gainfully employed but might jump ship if a better offer comes along and who possess specific skills that are incredibly hard to find. The perception (and there is much debate as to whether this is true) is that the best talent is not unemployed or looking. The best talent is employees hard at work for their firms using their experience and expertise in their fields—characteristics that can be transferred to new positions.

Where are most passive candidates?

LinkedIn.

When it comes to recruiting, it is one of the sites HR professionals trust most.

Although LinkedIn does not record these data, a 2013 study by SHRM revealed that 94 percent of recruiters said they use LinkedIn for recruitment; 54 percent said they used Facebook, and 39 percent said they used Twitter. "Less than 10 percent of organizations use other sites like Google +, YouTube, SHRM Connect, Pinterest, and Foursquare." Most of those recruiting through LinkedIn—87 percent—said they were seeking candidates for "non-management salaried positions; 80 percent were for management or director-level positions.[2]

In fact, use of LinkedIn by recruiters is so prevalent, that a 2012 study by Jobvite revealed that 93 percent of all hires made through social networking sites were made via LinkedIn.[3]

LinkedIn states that it attracts approximately two new members per second, and with more than 200 million members worldwide, it is the largest online resume database in the world.

"The world of recruiting has changed as a result of social media and mobile technology," Karie Willyerd, chief learning officer for SuccessFactors, said.[4] "The hiring process is no longer just about face-to-face or phone interviews. In some industries and regions, leveraging mobile, social media, and online tools is a regular part of the recruiting process. Companies that don't embrace these tools risk being left behind and losing the best job candidates."

Applicants who cannot access an optimized career site from their smart devices will look for jobs elsewhere, and an optimized mobile career site is not just a replication of what can be accessed from a desktop. It is one that allows candidates to apply for a job from their smartphones and tablets. It enables them to import their resumes or work history and references from their LinkedIn profiles and offers features that make it easier to submit other contact information—without having to fill out numerous pages on a smaller screen.

The Social Jobs Partnership, a collaboration of Facebook and other employers, reported in 2012 that nearly 90 percent of companies say Facebook has decreased the amount of money they spent on print advertising that is normally reserved for recruiting.[5]

Surveys studied and recruiters interviewed for this book revealed that hiring professionals and recruiters—especially those at smaller companies who cannot afford job boards—are increasingly using social media to find passive candidates (see Figure 6.1). The people who already have jobs actually make up nearly 80 percent of the available talent pool; about 20 percent of the workforce is actively looking for jobs.

To attract and find passive candidates, hiring professionals are also leveraging all of their networks (personal and professional) by tweeting jobs and sharing openings on Facebook, LinkedIn, Google + , Pinterest, Glassdoor, and other websites where people congregate. What's more, they are not just using traditional job boards like CareerBuilder, Dice, and Monster, or turning to Craigslist, either. Employers are seeking vendors that are closing the gap between social networking sites and candidates by integrating Facebook, LinkedIn, and other sites into their vendor relationship management (VRM) and CRM platforms and into

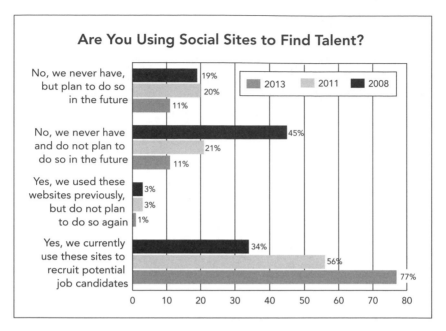

Figure 6.1   *Note:* Percentages may not total 100% due to rounding. Respondents who answered "don't know" were excluded from this analysis. *Source:* Society for Human Resource Management, 2013.

their applicant tracking systems. In addition, they are using tools that allow their employees to make referrals from among their Facebook and LinkedIn contacts. They are also being strategic about the use of social media by inserting source codes on recruiting channels to trace URLs, so they can determine how many applicants and employees are arriving from specific social networks; this information tells them where to concentrate their recruiting efforts most.

One of those places is LinkedIn. It has become the go-to site for recruiters and might likely remain so in the foreseeable future.

"Companies increasingly recognize that talent is their greatest competitive advantage," Leela Srinivasan, group marketing manager for LinkedIn's Talent Solutions group said in an interview for this book. "Our platform, tools, and insights make it easier than ever before for recruiters to find, engage, and hire top passive and active candidates and showcase their companies' talent brands, while reducing costs in the process."

LINKEDIN: WHY IT'S ON TOP OF RECRUITING

By sheer numbers, many recruiters and HR professionals turn to LinkedIn to find talent—for a lot of reasons. Available in more than 18 languages with users in more than 200 countries and territories, LinkedIn has become more than a social networking site for people interested in publishing their resumes. It is where talent is simply waiting to be discovered by recruiters.

To say it has become one of the largest players in the race to find talent is an understatement.

In 2012, LinkedIn earned $972.3 million in revenue—an increase of 86 percent from the previous year, according to LinkedIn's fourth-quarter earnings statement, published February 2013, and a LinkedIn spokesperson

The report also revealed that revenue is expected to range between $1.41 billion and $1.44 billion in 2013.

"To give you a sense of how dramatic this is," Josh Bersin of Bersin by Deloitte wrote in an article for *Forbes* in 2012, "LinkedIn's recruiting revenues are now greater than Taleo's [a recruiting company that was just acquired by Oracle for $1.9 billion] and within the year could reach the size of Monster.com. Monster's recruiting revenues were $250 million last quarter and only grew by 2 percent," he said.[6]

According to LinkedIn, among its 2013 priorities are helping recruiters find top talent, continuing to strengthen its infrastructure by delivering innovative products, and monetizing its products.

Only a small percentage of LinkedIn's revenue is derived from advertising. The website's business model is split into three different components: premium subscriptions, which users pay to broaden their use of the site; advertising; and Talent Solutions, which are the services it provides to recruiters who mine the site for talent. Talent Solutions is where the site makes most of its money.

Traditionally, recruiters used the "post and pray" approach to finding talent—they would post their job openings on job boards and wait for active candidates to reply.

Not anymore. Before LinkedIn, recruiters did not typically target passive candidates on a massive scale. Now, through its Talent Solutions platform (formerly Hiring Solutions), recruiters can use

Recruiter, an online software-as-a-service (SAAS) tool that LinkedIn gives markets to recruiting professionals so they can find, manage, and hire talent on LinkedIn. More than 13,000 corporate customers use Recruiter, and many of those corporations have multiple recruiters using the tool. LinkedIn charges companies about $8,000 annually for one to two "seats" or users of Recruiter. Some companies have up to 100 or more recruiters using the tool, according to a LinkedIn spokesperson interviewed for this book.

Other features of LinkedIn's Talent Solutions include Career Pages, Job Slots, and Work With Us. With Career Pages, companies have a chance to showcase their firms and position themselves as great places to be employed. Approximately 2.6 million companies worldwide have Career Pages on LinkedIn, according to a LinkedIn spokesperson. For example, visitors clicking on the "careers" tab on Nike's company page will see not just a listing of job opportunities on LinkedIn's site but testimonials from employees, too. Nike's page also provides insights about the company and a link to information about the firm's products and services.

When recruiters use LinkedIn to find employees, they are not just getting a candidate's resume or access to his or her connections. They are able to drill through a rich database resplendent with a candidate's skills, work samples, recommendations from colleagues, comments they have made on articles and blogs or within groups, or answers to questions that further showcase their expertise in subject matters related to their fields. They can also extrapolate information about their hobbies and other interests that may grant further insight into their employability and their behaviors. The site gives professionals a platform from which to manage their personal brands, advance their careers, and grow their networks.

Profiles on the site are easily identifiable. LinkedIn provides a window for recruiters into a potential hire's experience and lets them see recommendations. It is easy to search for talent and gauge whether those professionals are ready to leap from passive to active candidates—simply by their actions on the site, which may include increasing their visibility as subject matter experts in their fields by blogging on the site, updating their photos or professional experiences, joining and commenting in groups more often, or sharing their expertise to Twitter. Users like the site because they can find job opportunities posted there, share news items and e-mails, and network with peers, former colleagues, mentors, family, and friends. They can also conduct polls and get recruiting advice—some of it for free.

Thirty-nine percent of hiring managers and HR professionals have used at least one of the following tools to communicate with a job candidate: (see Figure 6.2).

In 2010, when Pinterest was founded, people used the site to create pin boards, adding photos of vacation spots, clothes, recipes, and other images they collected from across the web. Now people are pinning stunning visual resumes. Companies, too, are setting up camp with their own job boards on Pinterest. Candidates are making career-related pin boards on Pinterest and crafting online resumes on Vizify to aid their job searches, too. Pinterest, reported comScore, is the fastest-growing website in recent history, with more visitors than CNN and ESPN. By March of 2013, ranking service Alexa reported it as the 34th most popular site in the world.[7]

But in terms of sheer volume of users, no site compares to Facebook. Because so many people are there, recruiters are turning their sights to the site.

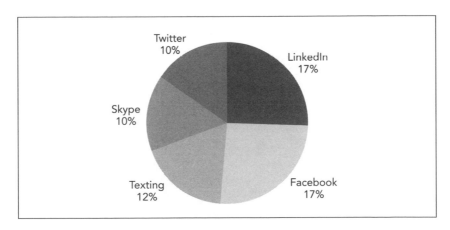

Figure 6.2 Tools Used to Talk to Job Candidates *Source:* Success Factors, 2012 *HR Fact-A Survey on the Pulse of Today's Global Workforce (South San Francisco-Success Factors, 2012).*

FACEBOOK ENTERS RECRUITMENT SPACE

A number of employers say they see Facebook becoming a more essential element of the talent acquisition process with 44 percent saying Facebook will become more important by 2015.

Because statistics show that people are spending more time on Facebook than on any other site, some recruiters who use social media say it behooves them to go to the site people use most.

"People do not go to Facebook looking for work," said Geoff Webb, a widely recognized social recruiting expert. "They go for photos, videos, friends. But if you give them an opportunity to apply for a job on Facebook, they will do it," he said in an interview at SHRM's Talent Management Conference in 2012 (see Figure 6.3).

In November 2012, Facebook unveiled the Social Jobs Partnership (SJP) app, a feature that allows users to find and share jobs. It partnered with the U.S. Department of Labor Department (DOL), the National Association of State Workforce Agencies (NASWA), the DirectEmployers Association, and the National Association of Colleges and Employers (NACE). According to the social networking giant, half of employers are using Facebook in their employment process, and "the new SJP app is a central location where recruiters can share open positions with the Facebook community sorted by industry, location, and skills." The app features "employment opportunities provided by

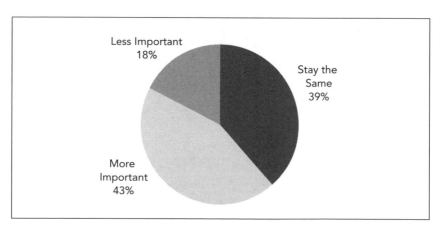

Figure 6.3   Future of Facebook As a Recruiting Tool. *Source:* National Association of Colleges and Employers (NACE), 2012.

BranchOut, DirectEmployers Association, Work4Labs, Jobvite, and Monster.com. Together, these developers are offering applicants access to more than 1.7 million jobs currently hosted on Facebook."[8]

Kay Calivas, managing director of Stephen James Associates, said social networking has helped recruiters broaden their "center of influence."[9]

Consider, too, that "a lot of people aren't on LinkedIn . . . but everyone you know is on Facebook,"[10] said former Oracle Director of Talent Management Strategy Steve Boese and creator of the HR Happy Hour Show on BlogTalkRadio. "Facebook is eating the web now," Sarah Patterson, former director of marketing for the employment website BranchOut and now senior director of product marketing at Salesforce.[11]

Employment experts said that Facebook's growth is the reason some Facebook users and recruiters are slowly allowing employment sites such as BranchOut, BeKnown, and Glassdoor to access their Facebook pages—and now that Facebook has launched its own social jobs app, expect social recruiting through the site to grow.

Although BeKnown, which launched in June 2011, would not reveal how many users it has, *SHRM Online* reported in early 2012 that BranchOut stated it had 10 million registered users.[12] AppData.com, which provides independent application metrics and trends, stated that BranchOut had 540,000 daily active users on March 9, 2012.[13] On that same date, BeKnown had a reported 9,000 daily active users.[14] Glassdoor, which just began allowing users to access Facebook in February 2012, had a reported 10,000 daily active users on March 9, 2012.[15]

According to a November 2011 study by Jobvite, which launched its social recruiting app on Facebook in late 2011, 53 percent of recruiters use Facebook because they see it as an effective way to get employee referrals.[16]

SHRM's 2013 study, which was referenced earlier in this chapter, reports that 54 percent of HR professionals polled said they used Facebook for recruitment. That number was 58 percent in 2011.[17]

"There's a huge audience of people on Facebook—people who you're not going to find on LinkedIn," said Tom Chevalier, director of strategic marketing for Monster Worldwide, which operates

BeKnown.[18] Once users access the app, it pulls in their photo, where they work, and their friends list.

"We don't bring in video or pictures. Newsfeed conversations aren't brought in. You're able to still use the Facebook platform, but you haven't violated the social norms that people have come to expect from Facebook," Chevalier said. BranchOut and Glassdoor work in much the same way.

BeKnown and BranchOut have special functions for recruiters who want to mine the site for passive talent. Glassdoor's Inside Connections tool allows job seekers to network with Facebook friends for referrals and to see personalized job listings.

"We did a Harris survey that revealed the two most trusted ways to learn about companies is through past and present employees," said Glassdoor co-founder Tim Besse.[19] With the Facebook feature, people can log in to Facebook through Glassdoor's site and see which of their friends may work at a company they are interested in and ask them "about the interviewing process, pay questions, or what it was like to work there," Besse said.

"As Facebook has become more intertwined and engrained in what people do on the web . . . there's a little bit more of a lowering of that bar between public and private and personal and work," said Steve Boese, who is also an instructor at the Rochester Institute of Technology.[20]

However, "it's an early time in recruiting on Facebook," Boese acknowledged, not just for recruiters, but for users as well. "Companies that figure out how to leverage Facebook as a recruiting platform are really going to have an advantage over those who don't," he said. "Over time, the ubiquity will be enough . . . to wear down the idea that 'I'm on Facebook and I should be private.'"

But not everyone thinks recruiting on Facebook will take off.

"I don't think most people want to network on Facebook—not with hiring managers," said Rachael King, a social media strategist and now at Sidecar.com[21] Although the developers of BranchOut, BeKnown, and Glassdoor said their apps do not access a person's complete Facebook profile, most people are hesitant to try them, King said.

"Most people have things on Facebook they don't want a hiring manager to see. It's just a personal network," she observed, adding that "people are already so wary, and this is coming on the heels of endless privacy battles with Facebook and Google—with them tracking you across the web. So many people are on guard about giving their information out."

Rules change, too.

"Companies can and sometimes do change their policies," technology expert David Davis pointed out during an interview. "New administrations come in, sharpshooters and efficiency experts are hired, and what used to be the company's policy when a user signed up for an account may quickly morph into a policy, agreement or terms of usage that look nothing like the original and we already know most people don't read them anyway."

Trisha Zulic, SPHR, director of human resources for an HR outsourcing company in San Diego, uses social media to find talent. She uses Jobing.com as a conduit to push positions she is looking to fill out to LinkedIn, Facebook, and Twitter. She then gets a Google Analytics report showing her how many candidates apply for jobs from those social networks.[22]

"The true measure of the quality of your social media recruiting is longevity," Zulic said. "Are those hires still in the job and performing well in year two or three?"

Some HR experts stressed that recruiters should remember that social media is simply a tool among many in the arsenal of finding good talent—not a replacement for it.

"I strongly believe in taking a multi-faceted approach to hiring," said Jason Hill, partner, Sound Advice Consulting Services.[23] "The old adage 'don't put all your eggs in one basket' still holds true for the use of social media recruiting. While I believe that social media recruiting has become and will continue to be an extremely powerful and potentially dominant tool for talent acquisition, HR . . . professionals must continue to use and keep other channels of communication open with their target audience. This should include employee referrals, multifaceted company marketing and branding campaigns, as well as traditional recruiting vehicles, such as career fairs, job boards and other sourcing methods."

Hill said economic conditions have forced recruiters to be "plugged in" to do more with less. "It is imperative that all firms have some sort of social and professional media presence for three main reasons:[24]

- Candidates are inhabiting social networking sites where they socialize and share valuable information.
- Customers and clients are also inhabiting those sites.
- "And this is where information sharing, trend setting and brand awareness will dominate in the years to come."[25]

RECRUITING FROM THE CANDIDATE'S PERSPECTIVE

While some recruiters are using social media tools to push jobs out to candidates and help them find talent, others are scouring the entire Internet for candidates' social media presence. They are scrutinizing not just their Facebook, Twitter, LinkedIn, and other postings, but what candidates are writing in blogs and in other places, too.

How are recruiters doing this? They are using tools like Radian6 and Talent Bin and other social listening tools to help search the web for candidates' social media footprints. They are analyzing candidates' skills and assessing their capabilities by observing their publically available conversations and harnessing professionally relevant information they have contributed online.

Are those candidates too expensive? Recruiters are then looking at their connections—their friends—and reaching out to them to see if they may be a good match.

Some candidates are put off by aggressive measures. For example, Android-code developers say they have been inundated with so many online employment offers from aggressive recruiters that they have placed notes on some of their social media profiles asking recruiters not to approach them. Others are commenting anonymously on blogs populated by code dwellers—a frequent stop for IT recruiters and hiring managers trying to find talent.

David Davis, a Philadelphia native who writes code for iPhone and Android devices, said in an interview for this book that the increased demand for experienced developers, is "as if you've filled out a contest form and somehow a bunch of . . . marketers have gotten your info. The next thing you know, you are inundated with offers for credit or others expounding on the large amounts of cash prizes you've already won."

"For example," he continues, "let's say that a headhunter places me. My salary will be $80,000 annually or better. At 10 percent of the placed consultant's salary, the person who placed me earns about $8,000. Can you imagine what life would be like for the person who can successfully place only two [people] per month? What about five? 10? These are big dollars for someone who is simply searching for talent and connecting [that talent] with an employer," Davis said.

Some recruiting professionals, including Joey V. Price, PHR, and CEO of Jumpstart: HR, and Gerry Crispin, SPHR, chief navigator of CareerXroads, said in interviews for this book that recruiters should consider recruitment from the candidates' perspective.

Be "candidate friendly," when recruiting, said Price. "In order to think like a candidate, think like a consumer. What factors would play into your decision when buying a car or considering a movie? Job search has the same premise. Think about what factors matter most in your decision, and make it easy for the candidate to match those things with what's on your website or within the links you provide on social media."

For example, be inviting, informative, and intuitive. How do you do that? Be welcoming in text, pictures, and video. Use inclusive language such as "we," "our," and "us."

Crispin, a board member of the Talent Board, which awards companies that excel at providing the best candidate experience in recruiting, suggests that recruiters considering using social media to find talent "speak clearly and consistently about the values of the firm, the requirements of the job, the relationship of the job to the success of the firm, the people who succeed in the firm, the style of the hiring manager, and the strengths and weaknesses of the team and other functions."

Recruiters should answer truthfully about the job and about the conditions of employment, too.

"Authenticity means sharing information that I need as a candidate to make a better decision," Crispin said. "Social is moving us into a two-way world of communication and when a candidate says they are interested in salary, a manager's style of leadership, what happened to the last incumbent in this position, etc., recruiters need to be empowered to answer in a way that is truthful and believable . . . because the candidate can get the answers elsewhere in a heartbeat."

Where?

Google.

"Deliver on the expectations you set" as well, Crispin advised. "Recruiters who fail to share what to expect in how a candidate will be treated in each of the phases of the recruitment process will be at the mercy of the expectations that is in the heads of every candidate at the moment he or she presses 'submit' at the end of the [online] application."

To avoid that, recruiters should talk to candidates throughout the courting process—beyond a friendly "we have received your application" notification once the candidate applies for a position. Hiring managers, too, should ask candidates about their recruitment experience and apply that information to future recruitment endeavors.

Recruiters should share company news via social media to entice employees to build their own brands within their firms.

A 2012 survey conducted by a Washington, D.C.-area HR firm found that job candidates in the U.S. look for one thing above all others when applying for jobs: opportunities for growth and professional development (see Figure 6.4).

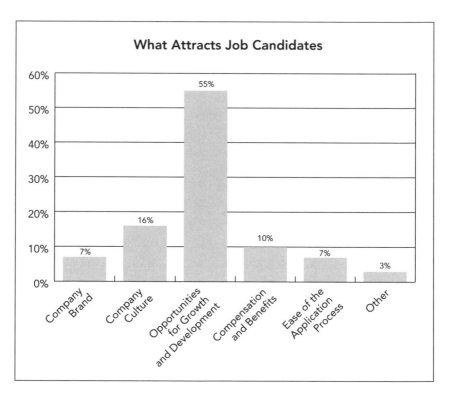

Figure 6.4   *Source:* Jumpstart: HR, 2012.

Price said candidates want to get to know more about "your organization, your company culture, about training and development, and what they can find beneficial from working at your organization." They also want to know if your company is stable.

Include links or badges on the company website on where to find the company on social networking sites such as Facebook, Twitter, blogs, YouTube, and LinkedIn. "Make sure your site—and the information provided within your social media discussions—has everything a job seeker would want to know about your organization before making a decision to apply," Price said.

SOME SOCIAL RECRUITING PITFALLS

It Is Not All a Bed of Roses: The Perils of Social Media Screening

Attracting talent through social media is a boon for those recruiters using it—even though some candidates may find the cold calling a bit intrusive. But one thing those using these channels to recruit should keep in mind is that using social media to find employees is not without issues—especially when investigating or scrutinizing candidates.

Fast Fact: 26 percent of organizations surveyed in 2011 indicated they used Google, Yahoo, and other search engines to screen job candidates during the hiring process.

By 2013, about 69 percent of companies said they have never used or no longer plan to use social networking websites or online search engines (63 percent) to screen candidates. About 74 percent of those surveyed said they were concerned about discovering information about protected characteristics (such as age, race, gender, and religious affiliation). About 54 percent had those concerns in 2008. Nearly half—48 percent—said they do not use social media to screen candidates because they could not verify with confidence the information from a job candidate's social networking page, as

continued

Although many recruiters are using social networking for recruiting, and the practice is increasing, SHRM's research reveals that "contrary to popular beliefs, it appears that only a small number of organizations are using online search engines and social networking websites to *screen* job candidates."[26]

Why?

Most of those polled cited legal risks, the lack of verifiable data, and the fact that much of the information found was unrelated to the job.

As one recruiter said, some passive candidates are often overlooked on various social media sites if their profiles lack an abundance of action words, lofty achievements, and connections with hundreds of friends, colleagues, and associates.

SHRM's 2013 study also points out that 71 percent of companies do not plan to implement formal policies within the next 12 months when it comes to using social networking sites to screen candidates.[27]

Some in HR are hesitant about using social media for screening, but research is showing that social media is becoming a great way for people to find jobs—especially on LinkedIn and Facebook.

compared with 43 percent in 2008.

In addition, by 2013, 63 percent of those surveyed said that information found on social sites may be irrelevant to job performance or ability to do the job.

Source: SHRM Research, 2008, 2011, 2013.

Employees hired through connections and referrals, including social networking sites, have a lower turnover rate than employees hired through other sources (see Figure 6.5).

It is a tricky subject. Experts say recruiters—at least in the United States—might be entering a legal minefield that could lead to thousands of dollars in fines if they are not documenting *how* they search for talent as well as following U.S. record-keeping laws prohibiting discrimination, especially when hiring federal contractors.

Recruiting and record keeping go hand in hand, experts said.

"You still have to keep records," Joey V. Price of Jumpstart: HR said during an interview for this book "Even if you are not a federal con-

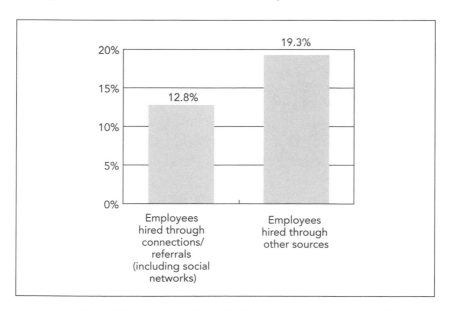

Figure 6.5   *Source:* The A-List, *Social Media Recruiting Effectiveness: Candidate Sourcing and Turnover* (Minneapolis, MN: TheAList.biz, 2012).]

tractor, there are still liability issues you have to consider—especially if someone makes a discrimination complaint."

Employers might open themselves up to lawsuits resulting from disparate impact claims.[28] Disparate impact refers to policies, practices, or rules that seem impartial but result in discrimination against members of a protected class—in other words, certain groups of people who are protected under nondiscrimination laws because of their national origin, race, color, religion, gender, disability, pregnancy, or veteran status or because of their genetic information. State and local laws can determine additional protected classes, such as sexual orientation and marital status. Readers should, however, consult an attorney on all specific questions pertaining to employment and labor law.

Some people view LinkedIn as the social networking site for people in suits and ties. According to the Pew Internet & American Life Project, nearly twice as many men (63 percent) as women (37 percent) use LinkedIn, and most users of that site have at least one college degree.[29] But, more important, about 85 percent of LinkedIn users and 78 percent of Facebook users are white, meaning that entire minority groups may not even be considered for positions if recruiters are focusing their efforts on those two sites.

Regulations from the U.S. Department of Labor's (DOL) Office of Federal Contract Compliance Programs (OFCCP) require federal contractors and subcontractors to collect information about the gender, race, and ethnicity of each "applicant" for employment. The sheer number of people applying for jobs online can overwhelm those charged with keeping records. Factor in the use of mobile devices and trying to figure out how to keep records on the devices, many of which have different Internet platforms, and that difficulty could increase, experts warn.

Running afoul of the law is not restricted to just the U.S., either. For example, in the United Kingdom, human resources must be concerned with the 1998 Data Protection Act, which regulates the protection of personal data.[30]

Companies often unwittingly "violate a host of laws when they use social media sources to recruit top talent, or when they use these sites to collect information about potential candidates," said David P. Jones, former global head of human resources consulting with Aon Consulting Worldwide.[31]

According to *SHRM Online*, Jones served as an expert witness in court cases related to hiring compliance and equal employment opportunity. Though he advises hiring managers to use social networks to recruit and screen potential employees, he cautious recruiters to do so with care.

"As in other areas of a business, technology brings a faster/better/cheaper package of payoffs to recruiting and hiring," Jones told the website "Just be careful, though, that how you use it doesn't bring faster/bigger/more-expensive legal challenges."

Be careful of "what your Internet searches or social networking reviews capture," Jones said. "Pulling information off Facebook, LinkedIn or other sites . . . outside what the job demands can lay the foundation for a candidate claiming they were passed over because someone made a wrong interpretation about their personal lifestyle information."

If you purchase Internet-scraped information about candidates, be careful. Did you know that doing this makes you subject to the federal government's Fair Credit Reporting Act (FCRA)? Jones asked.

"If a vendor tells you [its] recruiting or screening technology is legal, get the details. Review your overall recruiting and hiring program to find potential pitfalls, too. There are new laws, regulations, and court decisions coming down all the time," Jones said.

"The Internet and technology have reinvented how the best companies find the best talent," he added. "Drawing a payoff from making great hiring decisions always brings the risk of legal challenge. Setting up the right controls and training the people who use the technology is the best way to reduce [those risks]."[32]

Despite the risks associated with social media screening, recruiters are likely to continue flocking in droves to social media sites as more and more people spend time there.

BEST PRACTICES FOR SOCIAL MEDIA RECRUITING

- Be social and sociable. You cannot recruit where you are not present. Develop a diverse strategy for recruiting across all social media channels to reach a broader, more diverse talent pool. Many companies have erected a presence on Facebook, Twitter, LinkedIn, Pinterest, Google +, YouTube, and other channels. Others are using vendors, like iCIMS or Salesforce or Aventure, which have incorporated social media components into their talent acquisition software.

- Before hiring, decide which types of candidates you are seeking and what value they can add to the firm. Determine whom you are seeking and go where they are. For example, whereas more experienced candidates may be on LinkedIn and other networks, recent graduates will likely inhabit Facebook, may pin their resumes on Pinterest, and voice their opinions on blogs and Twitter.

- Think like a candidate. Consider how you got your job. Walk in the candidates' shoes, Gerry Crispin advised. Consider how many steps it took you to research your job, apply for it, wait for a response, and set up an interview. Then ask those interviewed about their recruitment experience, so you can improve the process.

- Monitor what your online search reviews capture or use software to screen social media sites to filter out protected-class information.

- Seek passive candidates directly or through their connections through their LinkedIn, Facebook, blog, or other public social media postings across the web.

- Develop relationships. Listening to candidates, engaging them in conversation, and developing relationships that may later lead to jobs is only the beginning. Their connections and expertise may prove fruitful in other areas as well. Social listening tools, of which there are hundreds, can identify candidates for future recruitment. Do not erect social sites and ignore them; and remember, simply using hashtags such as #jobs and #careers is not enough either. Pay attention to tweet chats (prearranged Twitter discussions) related to your industry and the people participating in them. Comment on blogs, too.

- Share relevant information about employment issues, current events, and statistics, and retweet comments your candidates say or may find interesting.

- Remember, social recruiting is not a 100 percent solution to retaining solid talent. Consider creating in-person events to meet candidates. After, all, everyone is not on LinkedIn, Facebook, or Twitter. Social media is only a tool in the arsenal for recruitment and should not be used exclusively for finding or sourcing candidates.

7 | Online Safety

One of the many reasons companies are loathe to let employees use social media is the risk it can pose to their networks, and HRIT professionals are on the front line of mitigating those risks.

However, research and experts reveal that the benefits of social media use far outweigh the risks, which include not only damage to reputations but the risk of data breaches, intellectual property loss, privacy violations, noncompliance with record management regulations, and the introduction of viruses, spyware, and malware into the enterprise.

"A company's need to maintain data security can limit the ways in which social technologies can be applied," states the McKinsey Global Institute. "In addition, in many nations, censorship and restrictions on Internet use stand in the way of value creation by companies that hope to enable consumers to interact with them and that wish to harvest deep insights from social data."[1]

In a 2011 study conducted by information security firm Clearswift, more than half of companies worldwide—56 percent—said they block access to some social media sites, fearing employees' activities on these sites might leave them open to data breaches or viruses.[2] In the United States, however, 30 percent of companies actively encourage their employees to use social media tools.

That encouragement could be because blocking access might cause friction between employers and employees—particularly young employees. Consider this: In many high schools nationwide, each student is given an iPad containing his or her assignments, and textbooks often reside in the cloud. Many surf the web in school to access information and visit social networking sites to complete assignments. For them, accessing the entire Internet—not just portions of it—is no big deal and really no concern. Today, an iPad, a laptop, an Android, or an iPhone, a BlackBerry, any computing device really, is as essential as a pencil or a book bag. According to Clearswift, 55 percent of 18- to 24-year-olds believe that they are entitled to visit social networking sites—while they are working. Moreover, according to a September 2011 survey from the Poneman Institute, 63 percent of respondents said that although social media represents a serious business risk, only 29 percent report having adequate controls to manage the risk.[3]

"Security is one of the primary barriers to social adoption," IBM's Sandy Carter said in an interview. "If an organization is ready to delve into social, but concerned about security, the first step to success is to choose a trusted partner you know can deliver a secure environment."

"There are always risks for allowing and promoting the use of immediate communication modes, but the benefits outweigh the consequences," Joe Shaheen, managing director of consulting firm Human Alliance Ltd. in Washington, D.C., told *SHRM Online*.[4] "The traditional hierarchical view of the firm is going away."

What is a manager to do?

EDUCATE THE STAFF

Anyone who uses the Internet should be aware by now that any online behavior is risky—opening popular news sites can be risky. So is visiting Facebook and clicking on a link in Twitter. Should employees be concerned about the potential threat of viruses? Yes. Should they be concerned to the point where they block employee use of these sites because of them? No. An educated employee is the best defense against data breaches and malware attraction. So are having robust IT security protocols.

"Unique malware variants grew by 2,180 percent, to 17,439, from the first quarter of 2011 to the second quarter of 2012," according to an ABI Research report cited by *SHRM Online* in December 2012.[5]

"Games, social networking, productivity apps, and financial tools are flocking to the mobile platform, and along with it, malware. Loss, theft, spam, Trojans, spyware, data breach, and aggressive advertising are some of the few threats facing vulnerable devices," ABI stated in a news release published online.[6]

Symantec, an antivirus software company, stated on its blog that in November 2012, hackers pretended to be a well-known social networking site and asked users to improve their security by providing their financial data. But that's not all. Users were asked for other personal information as well as the passwords to their e-mail accounts.[7]

Websense Security Labs suggests employers use advanced cybersecurity preparation and take steps to ensure their networks are secure because cybercriminals have found ways to thwart antivirus software, and intrusion detection defenses, according to *SHRM Online*.[8]

Antivirus scanning can curb infections, and if that fails, antivirus software can detect and eliminate spyware and malware. Encryption is another option. Companies that think they are under a malicious attack or suspect infection can file complaints with the Federal Bureau of Investigation's Internet Crime Complaint Center.

If employees suspect a link on Facebook has caused computer infection, they should alert IT. Personal Facebook users can install Microsoft Security Essentials, which can help remove viruses. You must be logged on to do so, however. Apple users are prompted to use an Apple security update.

As I've written previously in articles for *SHRM Online*, social engineering, or phishing and SMiShing, is when hackers fool people into clicking on links in e-mails or text messages or on social networking sites—any place online where they can install malware or viruses onto company-owned handheld devices or computers.

The best way to combat social engineering attempts is through training. Smart supervisors know that teaching their employees to exercise good judgment before they click on links anywhere online, including legitimate web pages, is the best defense against cybercrime. Employees should be mindful, too, of downloading mobile apps from unknown sources—especially on employer-owned devices. For example, download apps only from the Google Play, BlackBerry World, or iTunes stores. And even though most people don't do it, read through the permissions before deciding whether to download the app to help minimize the risk of infection.

Internet security awareness training firm KnowBe4 reported that employee training can reduce by 75 percent the likelihood that employees will fall victim to such attacks.[9]

"You can only do so much with firewalls and with intrusion detection and anti-spam and anti-spyware, but as long as the bad guys make an employee click on something, all of that is for naught because that one click can be the beginning of disaster," Stu Sjouwerman, author of the book *Cyberheist*, a primer for corporations looking to protect themselves from data breaches told me in an interview.[10]

"Social engineering is a billion-dollar industry right now; it's organized crime," Sjouwerman explained further. He added that hackers in Russia can earn hundreds of thousands of dollars annually doing this in their spare time. "And these guys are good—these are smart people." Employees are easy targets. "Anyone clicking on one phishing link could do major damage."

Changing behavior is critical.

While websites may change content on a daily basis, our online behaviors typically do not. What's the cure? Think first. "Be suspicious of everything. Trust no one. That is the new reality," said Grady Summers, principal information security expert with Ernst & Young.[11] Many people trust links they see on legitimate or social networking sites or in e-mails, but "they've got to realize in this day and age [those things are] so easily faked," Summers said. After all, it is relatively easy to get an unsuspecting person to click on a link in a spoofed e-mail, on Facebook, Twitter, or LinkedIn promising to reveal previously unseen photos of Osama bin Laden's dead body, for example, or some equally fascinating yet fake item.

"There are a lot of practical things we recommend," Summers told me in an interview. "Users should think about using a different computer for accessing personal pages, like Facebook or separate their personal usage from their business usage . . . and keep their browser up-to-date. They can try browser sandboxing," he said, which isolates the browser from the rest of your computer.[12]

Experts say changing behavior is important to security. Everyone should have a healthy amount of skepticism before they click on something. Even hovering over a shortened link and looking at the root extension and then Googling the topic instead of clicking on a link can go a long way to ensure employees aren't exposing their companies to data breaches.

"What we teach [employees] is stop, look, think," said Katie Johnson, head of marketing and client services for the consultancy Awareity.[13] "They should ask themselves: 'Is this too good to be true? Is this a scam?' You can stop this behavior," she said.

Although organizations have been addressing opportunistic cyberattacks for decades, Ernst & Young reveals that many firms are finding themselves the target of more persistent and sophisticated attacks.[14] These attacks have one objective: to acquire as much sensitive data as possible without alerting the company that an attack is underway, the report states. The effort does not end until the desired target is obtained. As I wrote previously, in March 2011, U.S. weapons maker Lockheed Martin Corp. was targeted by an indeterminate cyberincident.[15] On June 15, 2011, the Central Intelligence Agency (CIA) suffered a denial-of-service attack or (DOS), which is when someone deliberately tries to keep viewers from accessing a firm's web page.[16] In April 2009, cyberspies penetrated the Pentagon's $300 billion Joint Strike Fighter jet project, a costly weapons program.[17] That same year, a security checked of the U.S. air traffic control system revealed it was hacked over and over again.[18] The culprit? Unprotected folders and pathetic passwords.

WHAT CAN HR DO?

Be proactive and prepared and be knowledgeable about the potential for risks.

"First thing you have to know is that it is going to happen. Expect it," Damon Petraglia, director of forensic and information security services for Chartstone LLC and a consultant for the electronic task force for the U.S. Secret Service told me.[19]

Putting policies in place to help protect corporate networks helps as well—especially for employers who have a "bring your own device" to work policy, or BYOD.

Companies should limit access to corporate data that employees can access over their own devices, and for those who do, companies should encrypt data and put a policy in place that allows them to install apps on employees' personal devices that can locate, lock, and wipe stolen, lost, or missing mobile equipment.

"Lock, locate, and wipe is fundamental to any bring-your-own-device" policy, Robert Siciliano, an online security expert with anti-virus software firm McAfee, told *SHRM Online* in an interview.[20] "Not having some level of control over that device . . . is irresponsible today." It can prove financially detrimental to corporations, too.

Security experts said that corporations turn employees into human firewalls by training them to employ good online habits. They also suggest that, in addition to assessing their applications for holes in security, IT departments add a second layer of data security beyond firewalls by making data inside their networks valueless to hackers, and stepping up their authentication methods.

But above all, HR must be prepared for the inevitable.

"Vulnerabilities crop up in design, configuration and implementation," Daniel Uriah Clemens of Packetninjas LLC, an information security consultancy based in Alabama told me in an interview for *SHRM Online*.[21]

"Businesses need to know that while living in the digital world their business viability is based on the technology decisions they make." Good companies "practice practical security disciplines, both offensively and defensively."

Said Katie Johnson of Awareity: "The majority of data breaches are caused by or related to human error—failure to set up a system properly, unauthorized access, mistakes and errors, password security, social engineering. It is important for organizations to ask, 'Are all employees aware of changing and more sophisticated risks? Have we updated employees with situational awareness as more and more attacks target employees?' All employees must understand their individual roles and responsibilities for protecting sensitive information."[22]

"Good IT departments understand that strong information security programs do not stop upon completion of their risk management plans, disaster recovery plans, or security policies and procedures," Johnson added. "It is critical to ensure constant updates and plan reviews."

According to a study released by the Ponemon Institute, the average cost of a data breach in 2011 was $7.2 million—per data breach event.[23] Having a plan to respond to data breaches is critical,[24] said Denis Kelly, chairman of the Identity Ambassador Commission, which certifies identity theft professionals, and author of *The Official Identity Theft Prevention Handbook*.

"If the response plan is not developed prior to a breach, then all costs associated with the breach rise dramatically," Kelly told me during an interview for *SHRM Online*. He said companies should consider how they will handle both internal and external breaches.

"Internal is systems, structures or processes that led to the breach. External are the victims and the public perception. These components must be addressed in tandem and with a high level of coordination," Kelly explained, adding that "once a breach is discovered, there should be a reasonable time—96 hours—from discovery to notifying victims." In this day and age, however, having a contingency plan to deal with damage control is a good first step—especially since the 96-hour window may give the company enough time to assess the damage, it might not provide ample time to respond to comments or social media inquiries.

"Ensuring you have constantly reviewed and revised electronic-use policies, covering all aspects of employees' potential use of corporate technology is key," advised Andrew Marshall, senior vice president and CIO for campus apartments, the oldest student housing provider in the United States.[25]

"These policies have to be backed up with enforcement and education to ensure employees understand what is required and work within the guidelines," he said, adding that "most security risk, knowing or unknowing, starts with an employee—whether it's writing a password on a Post-it note [for anyone to see], using a password that they use on other non-controlled sites, allowing someone else to use their ID, or unwittingly introducing a virus or malware. Not much of this can be electronically mandated, so the first line of defense is policy and education."

So is monitoring.

Keeping a Watchful Eye

According to IT research firm Gartner, by 2015 companies will increase by as much as 60 percent their monitoring of employee behavior on Facebook, Twitter, and LinkedIn.[26]

Andrew Walls, research vice president of Gartner, said in a prepared statement that "the development of effective security intelligence and control depends on the ability to capture and analyze user actions that take place inside and outside of the enterprise IT environment.[27]

Analysts at Gartner cautioned, however, that employers must be sure to avoid ethical and legal issues, such as asking for social media passwords, which is illegal in several states and being considered for adoption in many more. They must be mindful, too, of discovering information that may violate discrimination and privacy laws in the U.S. as well as in other countries. They should be careful who within human resources is scrutinizing this information and the employees who can access tools that observe employees.

Walls predicted that "employers will continue to pursue greater visibility of social media conversations held by employees, customers, and the general public when the topics are of interest to the corporation. The problem lies in the ability of surveillance tools and methods to produce large volumes of irrelevant information. This personal information can be exposed accidentally or become the target of voyeuristic behavior by security staff," he said.

"Surveillance of individuals, however, can both mitigate and create risk, which must be managed carefully to comply with ethical and legal standards."

BEST PRACTICES FOR ONLINE SAFETY

- Be proactive, knowledgeable, and prepared for the inevitable. Do not just encrypt data; train employees about good online habits whether they are on a laptop, desktop, mobile device, or any device that connects to the Internet. Employees should be ever mindful of social engineering and bogus links. Insist they think before they click and use strong, secret passwords that combine letters as well as other characters. If they receive a suspicious link, they need to ask the person who posted it if it is legitimate (see Figure 7.1). If employees do click on something fishy, have them change their password immediately, and alert IT so a virus scan can be done as soon as possible.

- Treat all public Wi-Fi as a security threat. There is no such thing as privacy online when traveling and accessing the Internet in hotels, offices, public places, or cafes. Consider giving employees wireless cards or hotspots.

- Step up security and authentication methods on work-related devices as well as on personal devices allowed for work use. Although some IT professionals question the necessity, it might be a good idea to keep work-related devices separate from strictly personal devices—especially if work-related data contain your company's legal, health care, or financial information. Make data inside networks valueless to hackers (encryption helps), and have IT assess applications for security vulnerabilities.

- If employees are using their own devices to access company data, develop a mobile device policy. Decide whether company information will reside on the device, on company servers, or in the cloud. Inform employees that personal devices that access company servers where corporate data reside may be wiped remotely if those devices are lost or stolen.

DON'T YOU CLICK ON THAT!

Have You Seen What This Person is Saying About You?

www.yesifyouclickyouwillgetavirus.com terrible things . . .

Figure 7.1

- In addition to reviewing computer security logs, have IT departments add a second layer of data security beyond firewalls that extends to mobile devices. Consider encryption, and set access levels for certain employees. Security software can lock devices; identify malware, spyware, or viruses; and use GPS to locate a missing device, track its movements, erase the hard drive, and copy information to the cloud.

- Alert employees to be careful about what types of information they make available when accessing social networks—especially through mobile devices that can be lost or stolen. Remember, social media check-ins may give criminals just enough ammunition to develop a composite of a user's personal information for nefarious purposes later.

- It is generally a bad idea to ask candidates and employees for their social media password or to stand at their shoulder and look at their Facebook page. Facebook contains details that could lead to claims of discrimination or disparate impact (as discussed in Chapter 5). Know the laws in your state about requesting social media passwords. By 2013, several states enacted laws making the practice illegal.

- Keep browsers up-to-date; avoid buying apps on mobile devices from dubious, unknown or untested sources; and read application permissions before downloading apps on mobile devices.

8 | Productivity: Your Perception Might Not Fit Reality

I magine a world in which every person in every office is given a telephone and told to use it for business purposes only.

Period. Even in an emergency. Seems draconian, yes?

Yet, some employers—39 percent of HR professionals, according to SHRM research—expect employees to work around the clock on company-owned computers and handheld devices and not visit Facebook or use YouTube or Twitter as search engines, or use LinkedIn to search for people who may help them be more productive in their jobs.[1] In fact, the same research revealed that larger-staff-sized organizations, publicly owned for-profit organizations, and firms with multinational operations were more likely to block access to these multimedia platforms.

Not only should employers allow their employees to harness the power of social networking externally, they can and should use it internally so employees can elevate their performance, something countless companies are already doing.

Why? Because inhibiting employees' ability to access the collective body of knowledge that resides in the minds of those using social media—internally and externally—might be damaging your company and your goals. When people are stumped for answers, they often turn to others on social networking sites for advice.

What's more, as one study put it, companies that hire knowledge workers, those that depend on consumers for services, products, and information, and those that care about their reputations (basically, most companies) can benefit greatly from allowing social engagement. Many firms are realizing that and have begun to use social media tools at work to foster innovation and collaboration and to find solutions more quickly.

> **Fast Fact:** Although there is growing evidence that the ability to multitask can be trained with repetition and practice, BrainFacts. org also reports that multitasking capability declines as we grow older.

That has definitely been the case at IBM.

"Today, more than 130 communities of IBM professionals around the globe are collaborating virtually," IBM vice president Sandy Carter said in an interview for this book. "This has reduced the time it would have taken to complete projects, making the team far more efficient than without social tools."

The McKinsey Global Institute reports that knowledge workers spend an average of 28 hours every week searching the web for information, collaborating internally, and writing e-mails.[2]

As we have seen, the rise of social technologies will be among the most important tech trends in 2013.

Companies are beginning to see the value in social interactions, and more companies are using social task management tools within their enterprises to get work done.

One such company is Industrial Mold & Machine in Twinsburg, Ohio. This small company—with 34 employees—gave each of its workers an iPad so they could collaborate with one another from their workstations instead of using computer kiosks stationed around the plant. By deploying the social networking tool Socialtext from their iPads, workers are able to save time by reporting directly from their machines.[3]

Not only do they help employees collaborate better, these social tools, "when used within and across enterprises, have the potential to raise the productivity of the high-skill knowledge workers that are critical to performance and growth in the 21st century by 20 to 25 percent," according to a report by the McKinsey Global Institute.[4]

Marsh University: A Case Study

In 2010, Marsh & McLennan Companies launched Marsh University, (Marsh U) an internal social networking site used by 25,000 Marsh employees in 100 countries.[5]

During a presentation at the 15th Annual HR Technology Conference & Exposition in Chicago in late 2012, Laurie Ledford, the insurance company's chief HR officer, and Ben Brooks, the company's senior vice president and global director, discussed how the social networking portal allowed them to capture the collective knowledge of its employees through blogs, videos, and other social media tools.

Their "university" has allowed its employees to collaborate and find resources to help insurance and risk-management clients in more than 20 industries.

Marsh U started out small and began by getting "ambassadors"— people comfortable with social media tools—to lead the way in engaging and encouraging the rest of the staff. "We introduced the notion that everyone is a teacher," Brooks said. Using a 30-second video, human resources petitioned employees to share their knowledge about whatever they were passionate about. Employees initially did this through blogs on the Marsh U web portal site. "We told them, sharing your knowledge benefits you, your colleagues and all of us at Marsh," Brooks related. "We got people in right from the beginning. People began to be curious. It was the spark," he said. That spark led people to teach a variety of subjects, like how to run effective meetings. One employee turned out to be an expert in tribometry, the science of slip and fall prevention. "He was a consultant in Atlanta and he said, 'I'm going to retire in six months and everything I know, I'm going to put on Marsh U,'" Brooks recalled. The social networking site gave people "a sense of pride about what they knew." Today, those experts tap each other's expertise in various areas. The ambassadors in marketing, HR, and across other divisions, "helped people develop relationships," which led more people to participate.

Brooks noted that they did fun things as well, such as a photo contest to expand engagement. "We got over 650 photos from colleagues around the world," he said.

The recognition, whether from the photo contest or from the sharing of expertise, helped grow Marsh University. "People want to be recognized," Brooks said. In any social networking site that is open and transparent, Brooks added, companies should encourage their employees to be informed, connected, genuine with clients and each other, nimble, and flexible and to move quickly to deliver quality results. "Express your candid point of view, and encourage others to do the same," he said. "Have a constructive debate. If you disagree, speak up when you have a question or new ideas—even if it challenges the status quo. Be inclusive. Be open to diverse ideas and experiences, and backgrounds." Trust employees to be ethical, and acknowledge that they have integrity, he said.

•••

A TOOL LIKE ANY OTHER

"For many years, people used communities of practices to network and engage each other," Yvette Cameron, vice president and principal analyst for Constellation Research pointed out during a telephone interview.

> "Social networking sites like Facebook and Yammer mimic those communities. Consumer technologies are becoming expectations within the enterprise. That look and feel and experience of Facebook, the ability to get access to information and get side by side comparisons to information—like I can on amazon.com—well, why can't I find information and people as easily as I Google in the consumer world?"

As Google pointed out in its 2012 study, *The New Multi-Screen World: Understanding Cross-Platform Consumer Behavior*, people are no longer diverting their attention to one task at a time.[6] "We are a nation of multi-screeners. Most of consumers' media time today is spent in front of a screen—computer, smartphone, tablet, and TV."

"Multiple screens make us feel more efficient," the study said, "because we can act spontaneously and get a sense of accomplishment—this results in a feeling of 'found time.'" Still, experts like Carson Tate, managing partner of the Charlotte, North Carolina-based management consultancy Working Simply said in an interview for this book that it is about how you invest your time using external social media as a tool.

"If we look at social media as one of the tools we have to do our work—it's just like e-mail. It's just like the Internet. It's just like the phone," Tate remarked. "How are you intentionally and purposefully using that tool to get your work done?"

People are not just using the big three social networks—Facebook, LinkedIn, and Twitter—for wasteful purposes. They are using them to connect with customers, to see their habits, to figure out when to reach out to them, and to find publically available information to make connections more personable (see Figure 8.1).

The fear, of course, is that employees will abuse what many consider a privilege—being able to visit social networking sites at work—even though most of them can and likely will visit such sites from the smartphones in their pockets.

According to a 2013 study by IDC and Facebook, the top seven consistent activities men and women ages 18-44 engage in on their smartphones are checking e-mail (78 percent); web surfing (73 percent); checking Facebook (70 percent); getting directions (64 percent); gaming (60%); conducting "general" searches (57 percent); and sharing posts and photos (53 percent).

What's more, 79 percent of those polled said they keep their smartphones "on or near them for all but up to two hours of their waking day;"[7] and 63 percent keep their phones on or near them 23 hours a day! If we are sleeping and eating with our phones in order to stay connected, why do we expect employees not to use them at work?

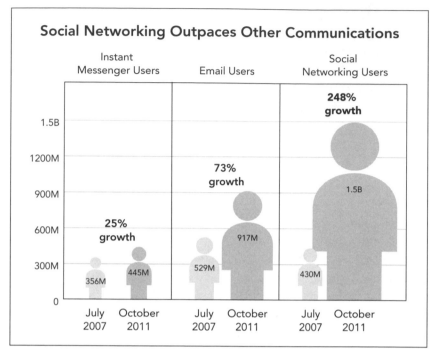

Figure 8.1 *Source:* Synthesis of comScore, October 2011; McKinsey Global Institute, July 2012
Credit: 2010-2012 Constellation Research, Inc.

"Three years ago at my conference, a young man got up and [asked], 'Would you tell me to leave my Rolodex at home [and] all of the people I know and I can call on the telephone?'" HR technology expert Bill Kutik told me during a phone interview

"'Well, you're doing the modern equivalent by cutting me off from my social network,'" Kutik said. "'My social network is how I get my work done. My friends help me with my work and by cutting me off from it, you are making me a less productive and useful employee.'"

Research supports this assertion. The McKinsey Global Institute reported in 2012 that using social tools to get work done can actually improve productivity when used to enhance communication, share knowledge, and collaborate and innovate within companies.[8]

So can revisiting employee-performance goals.

"Our research shows that companies which revisit employee-performance goals quarterly drive more than 30 percent more productivity than those which set goals annually," according to a 2013 report released by Bersin by Deloitte.[9]

Social media abuse is not a productivity issue, experts say, as much as it is a performance management issue. As long as employees are not introducing malware into your enterprise or divulging company secrets, you should really measure whether the work is getting done—not what your employees are doing on social networking sites. Trust and training on social media use go hand in hand.

MEET PAUL SMITH:
A NEW KIND OF HR PROFESSIONAL

"We use social media tools as a way to enhance our business acumen," said Paul Smith, director of human resources at the Delaware Valley Regional Planning Commission and author of the HR blog *Welcome to the Occupation*, in an interview for this book.

"So What If People Are Looking at Cat Videos?"

"Why would I want to prohibit folks from using social media? With training and development cost at almost a minimum or non-existent, you have employees who are seeking advice and information on the Internet through their networks. They're picking up on expertise free of charge for your organization. You want to limit that? Seriously?" asks Smith.

He adds, "So what if people are looking at cat videos? This is how we relate to each other. If you're on Facebook and you put up something funny about a cat video . . . you know what happens? You and I have a sort of different type of relationship. It helps us relate to each other. Then when we put something up that's more business-like, I'm more apt to pay attention to it because I'm relating to you from a [different] standpoint. That social component is what drives us as people—as a civilization.

"Let your employees tweet that they're eating a chocolate pop tart. Look at what they're supposed to be doing during the day in terms of productivity and if talking about a chocolate pop tart helps them get their work done . . . then don't cut off your nose to spite your face by blocking them from doing so."

Remember, too, that your employees are not just communicating with friends on social networking sites. Many are also getting their news fed into their social media streams. It is akin to picking up a newspaper or magazine in the break room in your office. "If I were having surgery on my brain, I wouldn't want my surgeon checking *The Huffington Post* on Facebook," Smith adds. There is a certain limit to what should be done. That would be extreme and unproductive, and again that comes down to performance management.

Employers may also fear that company secrets may be divulged by an employee's action—whether it be a snide remark or tweet or the posting of a damaging photo or video, all of which could cause a public relations scandal. But those fears have always been there. After all, an employee can divulge a company's intellectual property in an e-mail or by phone. Having policies in place on best practices governing business behaviors and expectations can curb those fears.

Measure Outcomes

Companies can measure productivity in many, varied ways.

Those who manage teleworkers have long discovered that managers can and should measure outcomes—not face time. When it comes to social media use and employee productivity, managers need to ascertain whether projects are being completed on time. Are goals being met? Is the work getting done?

"I understand the hesitation to want to block it," Jessica Lee, director of digital talent strategy for Marriott International said in an interview for this book "But if you're not making it accessible, people are going to find ways around it. They're going to use their phones or find other ways to be unproductive . . . people are going to be unproductive with or without social media."

After all, "employees found plenty of ways to waste time at work before the Internet was invented. Whether it's two-hour lunches, or happy hours, or cutting out earlier on a Friday or taking a smoke break, or chatting in the coffee room when the boss is out of town. It's no different than getting access to the Internet; it's no different than having access to e-mail on your desk; it's no different than getting access to a cell phone," leadership expert Ryan Estis pointed out during a phone interview.

"Someone who is disengaged is going to find ways to goof off with or without social media. I think it exaggerates an existing issue," Lee added.

Another point to consider is that banning people from social media sites could lead to unproductive behavior if they are worried about not being able to engage their networks during work hours instead of focusing on their work. Or they may find other ways to connect for their "Facebook break."

Allowing access to these sites gives employees the opportunity to "discover for themselves that they're not missing anything," Paul Smith added. "It's the perceived mystery and novelty that they're missing something" that actually hurts productivity.

"As we've grown up in the media age, we've gotten addicted to having more than one thing to keep us occupied," Geoff Webb pointed out during an interview Multitasking is a behavior that is not going anywhere. Consider, too, that if your employees are using social networking sites to produce content that will go to their friends' streams anyway, why not encourage them to help produce meaningful and beneficial content they can share with their friends that may benefit your company's reputation or add to its talent pool, Webb added.

Webb also noted one company in Toronto that encouraged employees to participate in a flash mob that appeared on YouTube. The video initially wound up generating millions of hits. "It was a great opportunity to get their employees involved in an activity that showed off their corporate culture," Webb said.

Trust Is Key

"If you don't trust your people, they're not going to reciprocate and trust you back," added recruiting expert Jessica Miller-Merrell. "They're not going to do their best work because they'll feel like they're in jail."

Ryan Estis agreed: "A corporation that worries that social media usage at work can hinder productivity is a company that doesn't trust their employees. That message to me is 'you don't trust me to manage my time, to contribute to the objectives, to deliver the result, you ask me to deliver.' That philosophical approach to business is an organization that's going to have a trust and disengagement issue anyway," Estis said.

Something else to be mindful of: If people are using a second screen (a personal smart device such as an iPad, iPhone, Blackberry, Android, or Kindle Fire) instead of their work computers, an employer may not be able to gauge or monitor the employee's activity. "We have no way of knowing whether an employee is performing to their potential or if it's a time management problem," Miller-Merrell pointed out.

"When you give people access and you let them know there are ground rules and parameters, I think there are a lot of great things that come out of it," Lee said. "People will monitor [themselves] and steer it into a positive direction completely unprompted."

Perhaps the biggest issue with allowing employees the freedom to visit social networking sites at work is lack of trust—and training.

After all, you are not hiring idiots. Why treat them as such?

In an interview with *MIT Sloan Management Review*, John Hagel, co-chairman of the Deloitte Center for the Edge, told the publication, "One thing that's really undervalued in discussions of social technology and social business is the opportunity to make the invisible visible. Companies need 'to see patterns of activity and interactions that you never knew were occurring.'"[10]

Whether employees are working in machine shops or offices or are hanging from utility poles, they can still use internal social networks to have colleagues weigh in with solutions to problems or to provide insight to help them operate more efficiently.

"Social media is not a distraction," Hagel said in a subsequent interview for this book. "It's helping us to our job better on a day to day basis."

Managers need to abandon the fear of risk as well as the fear of failure or embarrassment.

SOCIAL MEDIA COMES TO WORK

In five years, telling employees to stop networking socially will seem absurd.

"Go back to the Apollo Mission," William Tincup, SPHR, an HR consultant and co-host of the Internet radio show DriveThruHR told me during a phone interview. "We would never have put anyone on the moon if we hadn't overcome our fears. We are so fearful of making mistakes, but guess what? That's where the learning is and the growth is." When it comes to social media use and allowing employees to blend their engagement with friends, peers, customers, and colleagues, failure comes with the territory.

You have to learn from it and move on. Life is about risk and failure.

But your employees must be part of the conversations on social media to learn from each other. It is called crowdsourcing (see Figure 8.2). The Internet is filled with research! And whatever is not available on Google might very well be available in the minds or at the fingertips of the people in your employees' social circles. Those people inhabit Facebook, Twitter, Google +, and LinkedIn.

Increasingly, companies like Salesforce are leveraging social networking by incorporating social media tools into customer relationship platforms. Now, customers who post questions on a company's Facebook page, Twitter, or elsewhere on the web, for example, can be helped by a community of their peers and by customer service representatives—in real time.[11]

Studies show that increasingly people are multitasking more than they have in the past, and part of that multitasking includes checking social media sites, chatting with friends, sharing ideas, and collaborating. Sure, there are pros and cons about multitasking. But it can be managed. Nielsen and NM Incite report that 172 million people visited Google between January and October 2012; 153 million visited Facebook; and 132 million people went to YouTube.[12]

That same report revealed that people spend roughly 20 percent of their total time on social networking sites. What's more, in the United States, time spent on social media increased 37 percent to 121 billion minutes in July 2012, compared to 88 billion in July 2011.

Even so, work amazingly still gets done.

BEST PRACTICES FOR IMPROVING SOCIAL MEDIA PRODUCTIVITY—MINIMIZE DISTRACTIONS

- Tune in early, and check out later. Check social sites before work, and once or twice for 10 minutes during the day.

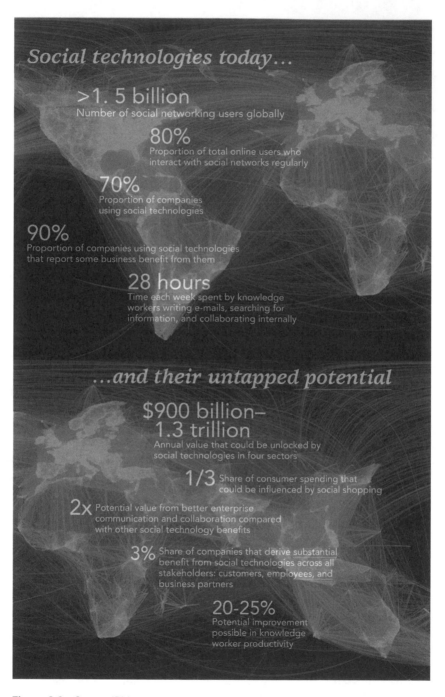

Figure 8.2   *Source:* IBM.

- Bombarded by notifications? Turn them off. Encourage employees to mute their phones and to flip them over to minimize Facebook and Twitter on their computer screens—particularly if they are on deadline. Check e-mail hourly instead of consistently responding to each and every notification. Make a concerted effort to manage the technology instead of giving in to its constant allure.

- Encourage employees to use social media with intent. Ask: Why am I logging on to Facebook? What information do I need to find? Am I looking for a client or prospect information? If not, go back to the first tip in this series.

- "Ask yourself if you have a fear of missing out," Tate suggested during a phone interview. Consider the need to check in. Whether it is the latest YouTube video or relationship status of your best friend, consider asking employees to shift that activity to a lunch break.

- Be patient with employees and yourselves. "It takes time to build a new habit. If you mess up and you checked Twitter 14 times today [and it wasn't work related], make a concerted effort to check it 12 times tomorrow," Tate advised.

- Schedule tweets and Facebook posts. There are many platforms, such as Crowdbooster, HootSuite, and Buffer, and others, that allow people to schedule their posts. Realize, too, that just because employees are attending an important presentation when their Twitter time stamp says they were tweeting—all is not as it seems.

- Trust your employees to meet the goals you set. For example, in a results-only work environment (ROWE) employees are trusted to do what they want, when they want, as long as their work gets done. Measure outcomes and the quality of the work. Are employees getting their work done? If not, consider their lack of productivity as a performance issue—everything cannot be blamed on social media abuse.

> *"Social media is now intertwined within the fabric of our society and culture, and there's no going back. . . . We have embraced social media as a major initiative."*
>
> —Henry "Hank" Jackson, CEO of SHRM

9 | Selling Social Media to Your CEO

In addition to writing the above quote in the December 2011 issue of *HR Magazine*, SHRM CEO Henry "Hank" Jackson added that SHRM made a commitment to ramp up its "presence on social media sites to communicate with you in the ways you prefer and to facilitate your engagement and interactions with HR professionals around the globe."[1]

Good companies embrace change.

Maybe your CEO has not jumped on the social media bandwagon. Or maybe he or she has just returned from a conference and has asked you to implement a social media strategy, but you do not even know what that Twitter thing is or how to use it.

Now what?

The best way to create an environment where employees are encouraged to use social media is to take a top-down approach. Often the issue is leadership and corporate culture. BRANDfog reports in its *CEO, Social Media & Leadership Survey* that as of January 2012, although 61 percent of *Fortune* 500 brands were engaging with customers on Twitter, less than 2.5 percent of those CEOs were actively using Twitter.[2] Moreover, less than a third of companies were using social media to mitigate risks or to enhance their corporate strategies.[3]

Action, in this case, can speak louder than words. But so can inaction. The easiest way to sell the use of social media by employees to CEOs is to have CEOs use social media themselves. (see Figure 9.1)[4]

But how does one do that?

Depending on your corporate culture, you could lead the charge and begin participation yourself. Or you could find out what your CEO is passionate about or what business issues keep him or her up at night.

- Is it employee retention?
- Engagement?
- Attracting talent?
- The bottom line?
- Growing the brand?
- Global expansion?
- Staying ahead of competitors?
- Keeping plugged in with business trends?
- Fostering innovation?

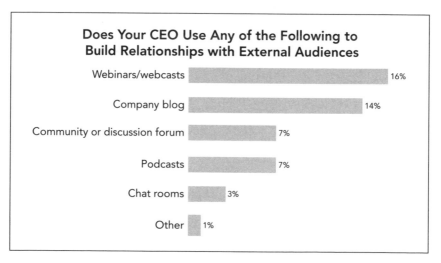

Figure 9.1   *Source:* SHRM Survey Findings: Social Media in the Workplace, 2011.

- Connecting with customers and clients?
- Sparking a fresh, high-tech image for the brand to attract new customers?

The good thing is that using social media can do all of these things by putting a company's best foot forward—internally and externally—and HR can do this by stressing the benefits of social media use. Once leaders become stakeholders in social media use within your organization, adoption across all divisions may be more likely.

Social media success is based on a return on engagement measure that can be ascertained by quantitative and qualitative outcomes (see Figure 9.2).

"Certainly for the C-suite there must be a [return on the investment] ROI," said IBM's Sandy Carter. "At IBM we're actually seeing the C-suite turning around and embracing social, she stated in an interview via e-mail.

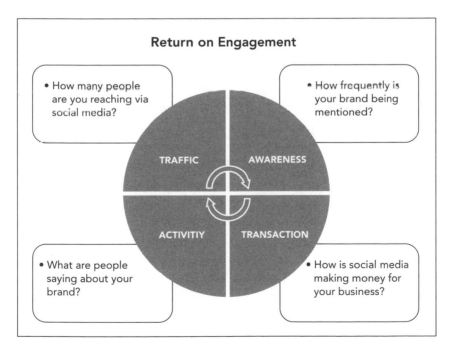

Figure 9.2 *Source:* Curtis Midkiff and Scott D. Ferrin, "Social Media as a Tool for Chapter Leaders," SHRM, 2011.

"For example," she continued, "IBM's 2012 CEO Study reveals that while today only 16 percent of CEOs are using social business platforms to connect with customers, that number is poised to spike to 57 percent within the next three to five years. Similarly, IBM's 2011 *Global CIO Study* of 3,000 global leaders indicated that more than 55 percent of companies identified social networking as having a strategic significance to their company's growth. And to round out the C-suite, according to the 2011 IBM *Global Chief Marketing Officer Study*, 82 percent of CMOs said they plan to increase their use of social media over the next three to five years," Carter pointed out. "So while historically social has been a tough sell, we're actually seeing senior leadership start to recognize and embrace its potential."

Fostering a culture of transparency helps.

"Transparency elevates trust," Ryan Estis, chief experience officer for Ryan and Associates, told me during an interview. "When people are informed, when they have confidence in the future, when they understand the position of other people, it elevates trust and emotional commitment. And social sharing and collaboration can drive transparency, openness, and connectedness into a business."

Zappos CEO Tony Hsieh told SHRM during a video interview in 2011 that "one of our values is about being open and honest and so we always try to be as transparent as possible."[5] "In my book, *Delivering Happiness*,[6] I talk about how we had to go through a round of layoffs in 2008 when the economy was bad and rather than kind of spin it . . . we basically had meetings and wrote this long e-mail that explained all the various reasons that we had to do what we had to do and . . . we tweeted out that e-mail and published it online."[7]

The company places a great deal of emphasis on pleasing its customers as well as on engaging its employees—roughly a third of whom are active on Twitter. Others employees blog or create videos for the company's YouTube channel. Not only has such transparent activity given its customers a window into its corporate culture, it has also enabled Zappos to communicate with customers and get instantaneous feedback. Hsieh, too, blogs for the firm and has more 2.6 million Twitter followers. He often tweets memos he has sent to employees. It is that kind of open transparency that has landed Zappos on *Fortune*'s list as one of the best companies to work for. Zappos was purchased by Amazon for $1.2 billion in 2009.

"I think any CEO that doesn't pay attention to social media usage by their company is in danger over the next five years; I don't see how they can be successful without it," IDC Government Insights vice president Thom Rubel said during an interview at an IT conference in Virginia in late 2012. "The technology is simply too pervasive."

Studies show that consumers believe social media can help companies enhance their brand and alleviate crisis management. Having CEOs engaging customers, clients, and consumers on social networking sites can help organizations position themselves as thought leaders in their respective industries and strengthen their credibility, too. Engagement is a two-way street. That means company's need to go beyond just reading, blogging, and liking something online. It means leaders from within their firms will actually have to start having conversations and not just broadcasting information. Consider, too, that not being in the space means not keeping abreast of industry trends or staying ahead of the competition. CEOs may be missing opportunities to glean insight not just from clients, employees, and the public (and the mistakes other companies make on social media), but from industry peers, as well. "This information—if properly harvested, filtered, and organized—can be used by decision makers throughout the organization to improve the corporate strategy, refine operations, or mitigate organizational risk."[8]

According to a study by social media advocate BRANDfog, 82 percent of employees were much more likely to trust a brand whose CEOs and top leaders were active in social media, and 77 percent of respondents said they were more likely to purchase from a firm whose values and mission were defined through the participation of CEO's and executive leadership on social media.[9]

In IBM's 2012 *Global CEO Study*, the company discovered that leaders are realizing that social engagement is how people relate to one another.[10] For the first time, IBM reports, "above any other external factor—even the economy—CEOs expect technology to drive the most change in their organizations over the next three to five years."[11]

Companies that ignore social media engagement are going to be left behind.

Why?

Social media sways influence and enhances networking. Look at it this way. There was a time when people you worked with 10 years ago would never encounter your mother or the people you went to elementary school with or joined a fraternity with. Social media has changed the ways in which our lives touch each other. This means, too, that our sphere of influence has changed dramatically—and rapidly. This change is not necessarily a bad thing. When everyone is a content creator and curator, our interconnectedness can enhance our personal and professional lives. Trust is essential. So is verification. Broadening our spheres of influence can affect a company's bottom line—not just through brand awareness and advertising, but through engaging prospective employees, recruitment, innovation, and collaboration.

But that is not all.

Through social media channels consumers, clients, customers, and employees are beginning to expect transparency and to be able to talk to and get responses directly from executives. And although C-suite executives may be wary about directly engaging without filters on social networks, "management competencies will have to be reinvented around a new set of principles including, transparency, integrity, collaboration, and consistent communication with stakeholders about company vision, mission, and values—through social media channels," the BRANDfog study points out.

Technology vendors are already crowding the space with new tools to enhance this engagement—especially inside corporate firewalls. In October 2012, more than 250 exhibitors and technology vendors converged on Chicago for *Human Resource Executive*'s 15th Annual Technology Conference & Exposition. Walking around the expo floor was a wake-up call. Almost every other vendor sold some platform with the word "social" in the title. In January 2013, research firm Bersin by Deloitte, said innovation in technology would grow as mobile tools and social recruiting systems make many HR systems in place today obsolete.[12] Employees will be encouraged to use these new tools to share information, manage their careers, locate experts, and network.

From a leadership standpoint, human resources must be instrumental in facilitating this engagement and in helping leaders align social media strategy so that it becomes much more than just hanging a shingle on Facebook and blasting out tweets to promote products and services. Engaging people through social media galvanizes them and makes them feel part of something bigger than themselves. Social computing and engagement when applied to business empowers employees throughout the entire company to be more open and innovative and can help streamline businesses processes. These tools can connect people who desire answers with the people who know them—inside and outside the enterprise—all over the world.

More and more companies are now harnessing the behaviors associated with external social networks like Facebook, Twitter, and LinkedIn to get work done at the office. As noted earlier, Marsh & McLennan Companies calls its internal social networking site Marsh University; IBM has Connections; Deloitte has D Street; and companies have signed on to use internal social networking sites like Yammer, Chatter, Jive, ThoughtFarmer, or Socialtext. Others are using these internal social networks to break down silos, benefit from collective wisdom, develop best practices, laud each other for a job well done, share content and conversations, and innovate up and down and across divisions.

According the IBM's *Global CEO Study*, 16 percent of 1,700 CEOs say they use social media today as a way to engage customers; however, they expect their use of social media to more than triple in the next five years, recognizing that social media engagement is the next wave of communication—and it is here to stay (see Figure 9.3).[13]

In a social media study released in late 2012 by the Conference Board and Rock Center for Corporate Governance at Stanford University,[14] 60 percent of chief executives polled said they used social media for personal reasons. More than 82 percent stated they used social sites to keep up with family and friends. Most executives said they were passive users, meaning they read more items than actually participated in back and forth discussions (for example, only 44 percent blogged, and only 20 percent followed others on Twitter). Use among boards of directors was low, too, with 90 percent stating they did not have a committee supervising social media monitoring efforts.

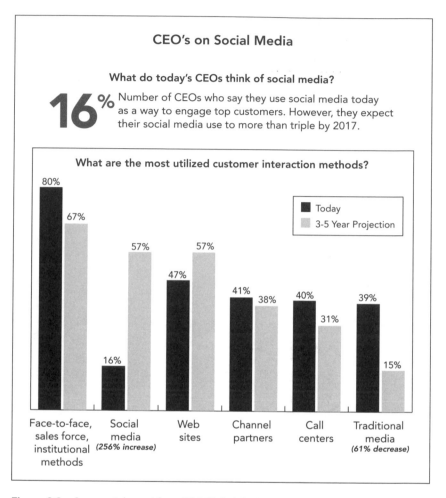

Figure 9.3 *Source:* Adapted from IBM Global CEO Study: Insights from face-to-face conservations with more than 1,700 CEOs in 64 countries.

As Enrique Salem, former CEO of Symantec told IBM, "Social networking has and will continue to significantly change how we do business. The way we collaborate with our customers will be transformed."[15]

It is already doing that.

For example, by using Spigit, a crowdsourcing ideation platform, global banking firm Citi got nearly 50,000 employees from 97 countries to brainstorm, submit, and vote on new products and services for customers in a "future of banking" challenge, *SHRM Online* reported in January 2013.[16]

From concept to product, what was once a process that took 18 to 24 months took only 10 weeks. Citi's initiative helped the company win an award from Constellation Research, which recognizes leaders who adopt disruptive technologies within their firms.

"Before the project, Citi didn't have a scalable way for employees to exchange ideas with colleagues outside of their departments or regions," Constellation's Yvette Cameron said.[17]

"Citi was blown away by the volume of employee engagement across the board, not just from certain titles or departments," she added. "That's the beauty of social tools like this. Suddenly you can capitalize on the experience, wisdom and creativity of everyone in the enterprise."

Not only are companies improving the ways in which they communicate through social networking—both inside and outside their walls—they are building their own knowledge repositories and improving their workplace communities internally as well.

DON'T JUST LOOK AND LISTEN: ENGAGE

Now that you have discovered what your CEO is passionate about, ask him or her to consider (if the CEO is not doing it in his or her personal life, like most people) using social media tools to read and observe and lurk among the peers and thought leaders within his or her industry.

Get the CEO to lurk first. Then have him or her engage directly with the people in those spaces.

"That was the step I took before joining Twitter," CEO of CMG Group, China Gorman, told me during a phone interview. She leaped into social media in 2009 when she was the COO for SHRM. "I started to read blogs that were written by and for HR people—people like Kris Dunn, Laurie Ruettimann, Steve Boese, William Tincup, Jessica Miller-Merrell, and Mark Stelzner—people who were really smart and were blogging about HR topics."

For Gorman, it became a challenge to find out what HR professionals who were not SHRM members were passionate about and engaging them where they lived and where they were active. She discovered that place was on social networking sites.

"I admired them. They were smart. They were talking about real issues [on their blogs]," and many of them were stunned that the COO of a company was sharing her opinions—unfiltered—on what they had written. "Every once in a while I'd comment and then I'd get a comment back," she recalled. Eventually, they encouraged her to take to Twitter.

"And I thought to myself, 'Oh, I don't care what you ate for breakfast. I don't want to know that you're walking down the street and it's a pretty day,'" she recalled, laughing. "And they said, 'No, no, no, no, no. It's much more than that. And that's when I got on Twitter.'"

From a business perspective, Gorman said having a presence on Twitter helped show that her organization was willing to contribute "to a community that we had not had access to or been engaged with." By April 2013, Gorman (her Twitter handle is @ChinaGorman) had more than 9,400 Twitter followers.

Other CEOs, like Zappos' Tony Hsieh (@Zappos) who had 2.7 million Twitter followers in April 2013 and Mashable's Pete Cashmore (@mashable) with more than 3 million followers, have jumped into the social media space with phenomenal results.

Gorman told me that she has found tremendous value in what she believes will someday become a traditional networking venue for CEOs. In addition to fostering community, CEOs must remember that they are humanizing their companies when engaging and talking directly with clients, customers, stakeholders, employees, and members.

Using social media, whether internally or externally, can help engage employees and customers in unprecedented ways. It helps foster a sense of community and mutual goals.

The critical thing to remember is to join the conversation in an equal way—not as a leader, but as a collaborative participant.

ADJUST YOUR CEO'S EXPECTATIONS

Ben Brooks, senior vice president and global director of communications and engagement for Marsh & McLennan Companies points out that many firms think that if people are not commenting on social media posts that they are not engaged. Nothing could be further from the truth.[18]

People are listening. There is an audience, and their engagement goes much further than a like, a comment, or a share.

John Hagel is co-chairman of the Deloitte Center for the Edge, a research center based in Silicon Valley that says it helps senior executives make sense of and profit from emerging opportunities on the edge of business and technology.

In an interview for this book, Hagel said the center has focused on getting senior executives to realize that social media engagement can be tied to metrics that matter—be they performance, financial, elevation of the brand, engagement, etc.

And if you can translate social media use to metrics that matter, he said, then there is more of a willingness to manage risk.

"We understand that there's risk here, but we understand there's real benefit," he said. "Too often the risks are something you can imagine and they're very tangible. The missing element is what is the benefit? Too often people assume the risk outweighs the benefit," Hagel pointed out.

Much has been written about measuring social media's return on investment—and it can be measured in any myriad ways. But perhaps the discussion should focus, too, on what companies are risking if they do not have a presence on social media.

For many executives, unfortunately, realizing the business case for social media engagement happens after something bad happens. For that reason alone, some consider such real-time, transparent engagement too risky.

"The thing about social media is it's in real time and companies cannot control the message," added NPR's Lars Schmidt. "People either [embrace it or] shy away from it, and lock it down—which is the case in situations of crisis. You can't control what's being said, but you can respond to it—but you have to be present in order to do so," he said. Even more important is if you are present and have built up a community of followers within the social realm, you already have champions for your cause.

"You already have a community, you may have fans coming to your defense, but if you're not present than you have no ability to quell that groundswell," he pointed out.

"I think so often in HR we are told that our primary job is to manage risk," noted HR consultant Laurie Ruettimann, SPHR. "So if you manage risk, it's important to get your head around social media and understand the multiple ways it touches your workforce in order to mitigate that risk because when you mitigate risk, you lower costs for your organization—if you don't understand social media you're not protecting your company against risk."

Understanding and embracing social media is imperative, too, she added because "you could be complicit if there's a lawsuit, if someone does something wrong."

"Resistance is futile."
—The Borg, *Star Trek: The Next Generation*

Consider also that no one division within a firm should own social media engagement. After all, if social media is good enough for marketing, public relations, and advertising—why is it not good enough for the CEO?

Still stumped about whether to convince leaders to embrace social media? Research reveals more CEOs are leaping to social media (see Figure 9.4). Consider this: Of all C-suite executives, CEOs were the best represented on social media.

BEST PRACTICES FOR MANAGERS ENCOURAGING CEOS TO WADE INTO SOCIAL

- Be the lifeguard. Just as a lifeguard scans the horizon to make sure the water is safe for swimmers, CEOs engaging in social media need to carve a niche in the sand for their brands and make sure everyone in the organization is in the same boat and can easily cast anchor. In other words, encourage your CEO to limit

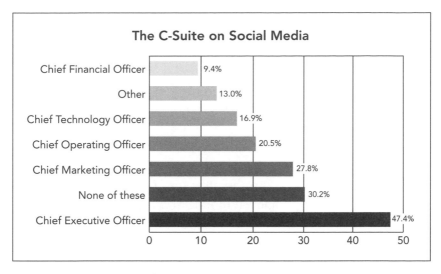

Figure 9.4   *Source: BRANDfog, 2012.*

the lingo and to make sure everyone communicates in like ways. No one person or department should "own" social media; all stakeholders—including the CEO—should be active contributors to both external and internal networks as well as equal contributors to its successful integration into your operations. When it comes to engagement, CEOs need to be approachable by everyone—colleagues, subordinates, customers, clients, and the like.

- Why is your CEO using social media? Answer that first before diving in. Then help him or her plan to gradually integrate social media use into existing work duties. Lurk first if necessary; target industry leaders and fans already in the space. Look. Listen. Learn. Engage. Share.

- Encourage CEOs to practice their ABCs—be authentic, benevolent, and *communicative*. Share links to videos to pertinent and interesting articles, videos, photos, studies, quotes, and advice. Have them ask questions and seek answers. If CEOs are writing blogs and posting them to Twitter, have them devote time to continue ongoing communication, which should never be one-way. Retweet others and have conversations with people. Sure, even the president of the United States does not do all of his own tweeting, but certainly CEOs can devote some time to doing it themselves, rather than leaving it to a PR or marketing team. (Obama occasionally does his own tweeting from @BarackObama; when he does, he signs his tweets -bo).[19]

- Develop a social media strategy to support your CEO's goals. Find it, and find an approach that fits. More than a billion people are on Facebook, but if your audience is not (unlikely), does your CEO need to be? What about Pinterest? YouTube? Twitter?

- Encourage your CEO to participate in social business opportunities both externally and internally. Seeking input from subordinates can improve employee morale and engagement and foster productivity.

- Target communities of interest. They are all over LinkedIn, Facebook, Twitter, and Quora and on blogs across the web. Engage with like-minded executives, leaders, managers, and others within your industry, and build on their collective intelligence to help you and your CEO increase not just awareness among peers, but to assist search engine optimization efforts as well.

- Allow transparency in social media conversations. The degree to which social media can blossom within your firm is directly related to how much your CEO embraces social media *and* is willing to loosen the reins on such engagement by employees.

- Find their voice, and use it.

10 | Why You Need a Social Media Evangelist

In 2010 a YouTube video of a Best Buy employee videotaping someone destroying a brand new iPad went viral. With unemployment at an all-time high, some people were upset and viewed it as Best Buy's sanctioning the destruction of an expensive device on its property.

It was early in 2009 when someone with access to Chrysler's Twitter account tweeted:

Source: Trisha Verma Re-tweet Chrysler Tweet https://twitter.com/tverma29/status/45483012326031360

Source: http://rack.1.mshcdn.com/media/ZgkyMDEyLzA3LzE5LzIzXzExXzE1Xz
QyNI9maWxl/ac5e2039

Chrysler apologized.

Aspiring journalist Cathryn Sloane caused a social media melt-down on July 20, 2012, when she wrote in an article for *NextGen Journal* that every social media manager should be under 25.[1]

She wrote:

> The seemingly obvious importance of incorporating com-forting social aspects into professional usage seems to go over several companies' heads. The typically tired com-mercial statements or aggressively slang-imitating phrases companies tend to use on their sites do not match the witty, honest, energetic atmosphere these social media outlets offer. . . . Yet, every time I see a job posting for a so-cial media manager/associates, etc. and find the employer is looking for five to 10 years of direct experience, I wonder why they don't realize the candidates who are in fact best suited for the position actually aren't old enough to have that much experience.

More than 600 comments were posted on her article, which was Facebook-enabled. Many readers took her to task, chastising her for assuming the only requirement for social media management was simply posting photos on Facebook and knowing how to use Twitter. One of them included the former director of new media for the U.S. Securities and Exchange Commission, Mark Story.

Sloane "didn't realize she was insulting an older generation of people," including potential hiring managers, Story said in August 2012 at a social media seminar in Washington, D.C., sponsored by Monster.

"Some of the smartest generation of social media people I know started out doing something else and stumbled into social media and started to figure it out," said Story, who, according to his LinkedIn profile, was appointed director of international corporate affairs for Alibaba Group in Hong Kong in September 2012. "We are at our heart communicators. We do subject verb and object and we try to influence and persuade. Facebook and Twitter and LinkedIn are just strategic tools to reach our audience. These are just tools, but you have to be a good, solid communicator first before you are able to do this."

Speaking from the audience at the same conference, Chanelle Schneider, a community manager at DeVries Public Relations and founder and moderator of #GenYChat, a weekly chat discussion on Twitter, added that social media managers "need to be able to understand marketing, qualitative analysis, and metrics. There's so much more to it than getting on Twitter and putting out a tweet and expecting the world to respond to it."

Embracing social media means being able to manage the good and the bad that comes from interacting with the public, and that means being prepared to hear what people really think of you, your product, and your firm, and realizing that it will not always be pleasant.

Perhaps more important is for employers to realize they need someone listening to social media conversations. Companies need to be part of the conversations so they can weigh in on comments, alleviate dissatisfactions, and address and resolves issues—especially from clients and customers.

It is inadvisable to ignore, erase, or try to sweep discontentment out the door or under the rug. Companies need to employ community or social media managers—people who monitor their brand, respond to complaints, and engage with customers, clients, and employees.

WHAT SKILLS SHOULD A
SOCIAL MEDIA MANAGER HAVE?

Good question. In fall of 2012, I posed that very question to HR professionals on SHRM's social media platform, SHRM Connect: "OK recruiters, what would be the critical competencies necessary for social media management? What skills would you want a social media manager to possess?"

Ronald Zornes, director of corporate operations for Canal Barge Company, Inc. in New Orleans, Louisiana, responded by commenting that ideal candidates would possess "excellent organizational skills."[2] They would be able to keep track of everything; be technologically savvy to keep up with new developments; possess good communications skills so they could communicate a strong and attractive social media presence; be knowledgeable about their company and their industry and understand and communicate appropriate messages that link to the corporate brand; and possess leadership skills to help establish and drive a social media vision.

Many companies are hiring social media managers—or they are outsourcing the function to agencies or consultants. Others are assigning individuals on staff who use social listening tools—software that allows them to keep track of and address problems people place publically on social networking sites, blogs, and other public spaces across the web. Some software companies have incorporated these social listening tools into their customer relations management or applicant tracking systems.

"We've seen a huge uptick in this new role," IBM's Sandy Carter said in an interview. "This is becoming a vital and skill specific position. For example, they need to be able to approach work collaboratively, they need to be good listeners, like to make connections, think on their feet and problem-solve well and enjoy interacting with others with a smile. Project management experience is definitely helpful when as well, but there are also many things that come up unexpectedly and social media and community managers need to be ready to shift and adapt the plan as needed which can be challenging for people too vested in a formal project management approach."

Maggie McGary was a former online community and social media manager for the American Speech-Language-Hearing Association until the end of 2012 when she left to become a digital content manager for a Federal Drug Administration (FDA) contractor. She said in an interview for this book that social media managers have to be able to multitask, do their jobs, and keep up with what is going on within social media because "it moves so quickly. With social, you're constantly reading; stuff is constantly changing; new tools are cropping up every day and keeping up with trends and the sheer volume of information can be daunting because it changes so quickly. I spent a ton of time online and I read a ton of stuff and it helped to keep up with everything." She paid close attention to her Twitter followers and other social connections, who helped her keep up with trends in real time.

Social media managers also aid in the development and implementation of their firm's social media strategies and campaigns, and may analyze search engine optimization and Google Analytics reports as well as train and encourage employees who use social media. Social media managers may sit in the company's marketing, sales, IT, or public relations department, but often they work in human resources.

While some companies are hiring or promoting staff from within the ranks to work as social media or community managers, others are outsourcing the function. Some are employing technologies like Social Mention, ExactTarget, Radian6, or those provided by Jive or Brandwatch to monitor social media conversations about their companies, but nothing beats a real, live person when responding to complaints—and increasingly, human resources is being tasked with this function.

Between May 2011 and August 2011, more than 1,000 new ads for HR occupations have included requirements for social media skills, nearly a 160 percent increase over the same period in 2010, according to WANTED Analytics.[3]

WANTED reports that some companies are looking for HR managers who have experience with social media management and who can coach employees to handle this task. They also want them to have experience writing and proofing web content and the ability to use social media platforms.

But what makes a good social media manager?

Being "a good listener, first because . . . social media is like going to a cocktail party, where there are circles of groups of people," Mark Story said at the Monster seminar. "You don't just walk up and take over the conversation. You sidle up and see where it's going on and participate in that social circle. That's the same way in social media. You have to be able to listen to what's going on in order to effectively participate in the conversation."

Other competencies include being a good storyteller and a good writer and possessing intellectual curiosity. "And you have to want to learn all the time. Even if Pinterest isn't for [you] you have to take a look at it and see if it is. Look at the latest failures, too, like Empire Avenue."

Social media managers have to be sociable, too. "You have to have really good communications skills in both listening and talking to people and talking in different languages—whether it's in 140 characters, a status update, or in a message thread," Story added. "You have to really be a solid communicator and be willing to learn about new platforms."

While monitoring what is being said can be as simple as setting up a Google alert or using social listening tools, engagement is different. It means being empowered to respond to customer or employee concerns in a nonconfrontational way—hopefully before the media or bloggers find out.

Social media managers should partner with a company's corporate communications and legal teams, so they can set parameters for what can be addressed—without having to get every single tweet and Facebook update approved. If social media managers are not allowed to respond in a very natural way, they should not be on social media sites representing their firms because trust is essential.

Let me repeat that. Trust is essential.

Brand management—and making sure employees are not damaging the brand—is a critical element as well. A good social media policy and training on that policy are also important.

IT'S THE POLICY, STUPID

The specifics of that policy "are vital," Bruce Kneuer, Kenexa's social media manager, said in an interview before the company was swallowed up by IBM in 2012.

"I've got 3,000 colleagues around the world from 15 different countries. The policy is universal. It extends to all of them." He said he has become aware of their social footprint "and I'm aware of their social presence. Now, they are not representing the company, but they are my colleagues; what they say and how they say it is a new phenomenon because it's so wide reaching and so easy" for the wrong thing to be said online that could connect an employee to a company and cause ensuing fallout.

It is a new world order. In March 2013, I spoke to HR professionals in Maryland on the value of using social media in the workplace, and they wondered why they were turning their employees into marketers. But, when you think about it, social media makes all of us just that. The fact is, when we engage in social media—even if we do so from behind the comfort of a privacy setting—we can become the face of our company, whether we want to or not; whether we like it or not.

Kneuer agreed with me. We are "not here to aggravate our co-workers or get anyone in trouble," Kneuer said. "But you are now speaking in ways that a decade ago no one would have heard you. Now you can be heard. So be sensitive. Given the volume of expression, people are playing nicely, but we still have to be aware that these technologies" can get us into trouble if we do not watch what we say online, Kneuer added. Social media managers should be essential in helping create or administer the social media training for employees as well.

HIRING FROM WITHIN

Social media management is not an exact science. A number of companies have discovered their social media managers from within their ranks—these are people who took the initiative to jump into social during its infancy. From seasoned marketing professionals to secretaries, human resources has been tasked with training social media managers or deciding the criteria for the position. In addition to having the aforementioned skills, some employers are considering candidates' social media influence, too. How are employers measuring that? By noting the level of engagement by looking at candidates' Klout scores or by viewing how many Twitter followers they have and how often their posts are tweeted or retweeted, liked, or seen by their connections.

But when assessing those characteristics, HR professionals recruiting social media managers must also consider the quality of those connections—not quantity. It is one thing, after all, to have 100,000 Twitter followers—but another if those followers are not related to the industry in which the person is working.

Smart companies are there to monitor what is going on. Some are employing social media managers to do it, and those managers are using reporting tools from vendors like Radian6, TMP Worldwide, Sprout Social, and Kred—as well as Facebook's Insights dashboard and Twitter's analytics tools. These tools measure a person's "influence" or "reach."

Online collaboration tools are broadening our horizons and social tools, and the people charged with listening and engaging will become a critical force in the way we do business in the future.

Leaders need to be on board with social media engagement—especially in the enterprise. Doing so gives people a chance to express their opinions, which in turn, elevates engagement.

TIPS ON RETAINING A SOCIAL MEDIA MANAGER

Let's say you define the competencies necessary for your social media strategy. Social media or community managers are tasked with fulfilling that strategy, driving visibility, and increasing brand recognition and engagement across social media networks. "You can know the tools and know Facebook inside and out, but do you know the federal government's rules for Facebook in advertising?" Mark Story asks. "Do you know legal, crisis communications, do you have management skills?"

To do that social media managers must:

• Be curious, passionate, thoughtful, considerate, approachable, attentive, genuine, helpful, and able to handle the stress that may come from managing different communities across multiple platforms. Day and night.

- Possess leadership skills to help establish and drive a social media vision that elevates the company's objectives—whether it is to increase brand or image awareness or improve social media engagement among employees, customers, and key stakeholders. This person can help different departments as they collaborate on social media engagement—internally and externally. Social media engagement should not be the responsibility of one department. For best results, your corporate culture may need a makeover to accommodate a shared, collective approach to its use.
- Be well read to keep up with social media developments and trends and be able to write and edit succinctly and informally—and be well organized to keep track of content on multiple platforms.
- Be able to generate reliable and relevant content that flows well across social channels and be allowed to respond judiciously during a crisis.
- Be as sociable as they are well organized to keep track of conversations and address issues and drive engagement.
- Be able to communicate appropriate messages that flow well across social channels and be ready to participate in relevant communities of practice within social networking sites to tap into the wealth of knowledge other community managers may possess.
- Be fluent in tools that help report and analyze social media metrics, search engine optimization to gauge the effectiveness of social media content, and company initiatives that affect marketing or public relations campaigns.
- Be able to provide insight, guidance, and encouragement to fellow employees across the organization to expand a company's adoption of social media.
- Human resources should also cultivate more than one social media evangelist. Succession planning is critical so one person does not hold the keys to the social kingdom if the main social media manager gets sick, quits, or gets burnt out.

> *"In a nutshell, when two or more employees discuss the terms and conditions of employment in a way that's designed or intended to effect change . . . they have the right to do that"—even on a social networking site.*
>
> —Eric B. Meyer, labor attorney, Dilworth Paxson LLP

11 | Rules Are Rules

Guess what?

People are not perfect, and they make mistakes. Fortunately social media mishaps are becoming less common.

When companies encourage employees to use social media tools for their own personal and professional benefit, they should expect the unexpected and plan for it. It is not enough to say, "Well, we just can't take the risk."

Well, you have not lived if you have not taken a risk.

Each time you get in a car or step on an airplane, there is a chance of equipment failure or an accident. Yet, we do those things every day anyway because, for us, the risk is worth it.

Approach social media engagement for employees the same way, and encourage employees to consider their online postings part of their "personal brand." People tend to take seriously what they write online when they know those posts may affect their personal reputations—whether those posts are public or not.

Fast Fact: Only 31 percent of employees work for companies that have policies on social media use, and even if a policy is in place, only one in four people (25 percent) use social media applications during the workday.[1]

YOU CAN'T CONTROL EVERYTHING...

Even though good social media policies and trainings convey that employees should be "fair, courteous and respectful," we know that human interaction deviates from this on a regular basis. Plus, the National Labor Relations Board (NLRB) has ruled that employees are allowed certain leeway in their social media postings.

It all began with the Facebook Firing Case.

In 2009, paramedic Dawnmarie Souza reportedly decided to vent about her boss on her private Facebook page, which she did on her own computer on her own time. She was fired after posting the negative comments in which she used a few profane words, called her boss "a scumbag," and referred to him as a mental patient. Her employer, American Medical Response of Connecticut, Inc., claimed she violated the company's blogging and Internet posting policy that kept its workers from making disparaging statements online about the company and its workers.[2]

Souza's case created a larger debate about whether what she had done was considered "protected concerted activity"; in other words, did she have the right to speak out about the conditions of her employment with her colleagues—using Facebook as a vehicle.

The answer is yes, according to the board.

After its investigation, the NLRB ruled not only that Souza was fired unlawfully because her posts, on which other colleagues commented, were protected concerted activity, but that her company's employee handbook was in error as well. The company later settled with Souza and changed its handbook.

Several other related cases have come before the NLRB, and as of 2012, it ruled that the National Labor Relations Act (NLRA) extends to *all* workers, *whether they are in unions or not*, and that those employees are allowed to communicate with each other about issues relating to their employment as long as the communication falls within the realm of protected concerted activity.

Social media just broadens that ability.

As *HR Magazine* reported in August 2012, "In nonunion shops, employers can still include policies in employee handbooks that prohibit workers from engaging in activities or communications that damage the company and its reputation. Individual gripes and complaints not made in relation to group activity among employees are not protected."[3]

"If I go too far, say things that are extremely negative, or challenge the quality of the product or services, I can be terminated. But if I say something that relates to the terms and conditions of employment, it will be protected," Charles B. Craver, a law professor at George Washington University Law School in Washington, D.C., told the magazine.

...BUT YOU CAN STILL HAVE A POLICY

Whether employees realize it or not, when they are engaging on social networking sites as individuals, they might be representing their companies—depending on what they say and the context in which they say it. Some companies require employees to add that their opinions are their own either in the bios of their social profiles or at the end of their posts to distinguish that what they say doesn't necessarily reflect their company's sentiment. Human resources can encourage online collaboration, but guidelines and company policy can put rules in place that can help employees be productive and keep them out of trouble.

It sounds like the simplest thing: Tell your employees they are not to discuss online such things as the company's finances or disclose proprietary or sensitive information. Yet, many companies do not have social media policies telling employees just that, and some may erroneously believe that what is printed in their employee handbooks is simply enough.

It is not.

Many employers have erred by making such policies too restrictive and have violated some federal laws, including the NLRA and the Stored Communications Act, which grants people the right to privacy.

Expecting employees to behave with common sense and telling them to are two totally different things. People sometimes act childishly when they are engaging others online. They type words on a screen they would not dare say to another person out loud—especially if they think no one who matters will see it.

What's more, as we have established, anything posted online lasts forever and can be misconstrued, taken out of context, and placed under scrutiny. Although having a social media policy is not required by law, and some employers rely on various other policies, such as antiharassment policies, I firmly believe you need a social media policy. When it comes to instituting that policy, employers should not just disseminate a handbook and ask employees to sign documentation saying they have read it. They should train employees on the social media policy as well.

"Whether you're allowing employees to dive into social internally or externally," companies should "set guidelines and values they can follow," said IBM's Sandy Carter. "At IBM, we created the IBM Social Computing Guidelines to set standards for every IBMer over any and every social media platform, internal or external." The guidelines are available to the public. A policy blessed by the NLRB is included in this chapter, but you can take a peek at IBM's guidelines, which it has made available to the public on its blog.

FIRST THINGS FIRST:
DEFINE A SOCIAL MEDIA STRATEGY

Before devising a policy, companies should first decide what their social media strategy should be. However, even if your company is not going to use social media, you still need a policy.

Why?

Because your employees are using social media—whether you want them to or not, and they will need guidelines to protect your interests and your reputation (and theirs). Now, if your company is going to use social media, decide who will use it and for what purposes. Will it be restricted to just a few people, say those in marketing, HR,

"I believe that culture is everyone's job," said Zappos CEO Tony Hsieh.[4] "It's not me dictating what the culture should be . . . and it's always evolving.

"We don't really have a process for evolving the culture," he said. "Really all we have are 10 core values at Zappos and employees are encouraged to really go with whatever idea they have as long as it's not conflicting with our 10 core values." Part of the reason for the buy in, he said, is because the values were created with input from employees.

or media relations? Or, as I encourage, will all staff be able to use it (internally or externally) as a part of their work and to further the corporate brand as well as their own personal brands? Are you going to require supervisors or department heads to know which networks folks are using? Draw up the policy with the firm's culture and industry in mind because some industries (financial and health, for example) have certain rules about social media engagement and what things can and cannot be divulged. Your strategic approach will need to align with your company's culture. Is it formal or informal?

For example, Zappos' social media policy is just seven words long: "Be Real and Use Your Best Judgment."

In addition to tapping different divisions (marketing, IT, HR, media, legal) to help craft the policy, take a look at the existing employee handbook to see which rules within it can apply to the social media policy (for example, rules on the code of conduct or the disclosure of proprietary information or sexual harassment or the equipment use policy may be applicable). Make sure the social media policy is consistent with and works in tandem with what is in the handbook—and that it covers postings on the Internet in social media platforms or technologies that exist or have yet to be created.

Sample introduction: Although the world of social media is constantly changing, this policy works in conjunction with (insert other

Fast Fact: "The overriding conclusion is that employers should—whether mandatory or not—put workable, pragmatic social media policies in place so that everyone—employers and employees alike—is clear on what is and is not acceptable and expected of them when it comes to the use of social media in the workplace."[6]
—Baker & McKenzie, global study of social media

policies) and is intended to cover staff participation in all forms of communicating or posting information or content to the Internet, including but not limited to social networking sites (name the sites), and other forms of online dialogue.[5]

....

YOU NEED A SOCIAL MEDIA POLICY— THIS IS HOW YOU CREATE ONE

A sample policy, written by Wal-Mart[7] and taken from SHRM's website, it was ruled lawful by the NLRB in May 2012 in its Operations Management Memo. This policy is probably one of the best starting points from which to create your own.

"You have to have a good social media policy," said NPR's Lars Schmidt during a phone interview for this book. "You have to have clear guidelines on what employees should and should not be doing on social media and hopefully they are grounded in practicality and trust."

Be Specific

Some attorneys interviewed for this book say the Wal-Mart policy is a good starting point for devising a policy—and employers can use it as a guide—but employers may want to be specific in some areas of the policy by using examples, again without frightening employees from exercising their rights to engage in what the NLRB calls "concerted activities for the purpose of collective bargaining or other mutual aid or protection."[8]

For example, "the NLRB has had a problem with companies that say you are not allowed to disclose confidential information without defining what 'is confidential information,' " Michael Schmidt, an attorney with Cozen O'Connor's labor and employment group and author of the *Social Media Employment Law Blog* told me in an interview for this book

"Some companies consider salary and wage information confidential and the NLRB has said employees can talk about wages—so a company would be overreaching by prohibiting employees from discussing wage-related information," Schmidt said.

But before devising a social media policy, Eric Meyer, a partner in the labor employment law group of Dilworth Paxson LLP, said companies should first decide what they hope to get out of social media (i.e., strategize), and their policies should speak to anything employees publish on the Internet, including comments on Facebook, LinkedIn, Twitter, Foursquare, blogs, wikis, online discussion boards, Google groups, Tumblr, and video- and photo-sharing sites like YouTube and Flickr because "any of that could impact the company."

"If you make it a rule, you may violate the [U.S.] National Labor Relations Act," Meyer explained. "Under the National Labor Relations Act, employees have the right to engage in protected concerted activity. In a nutshell, when two or more employees discuss the terms and conditions of employment in a way that's designed or intended to effect change . . . they have the right to do that."

But recently, Facebook has begun to show users who posts things in groups or pages how many people have actually seen their posts. Does this practice create protected concerted activity?

"I would say viewing a post does not create protected concerted activity," Meyer said. "This is because protected concerted activity generally requires two or more employee acting together to improve wages or working conditions. Although a single employee can technically engage in protected concerted activity, he or she must involve other co-workers before acting. I suppose; however, that if one employee merely 'likes' another co-worker's Facebook status update about improving conditions at work, that could be protected concerted activity," he added.

"Again, however, where the NLRB has really cracked down in the last six months [between June 2012 and January 2013] is policy language that is broad enough such that an employee could view the policy language as chilling their right to engage in PCA. Examples would include: restrictions on employee criticism of the company and confidentiality language prohibiting discussion of wages and benefits," Meyer said.

DON'T ASK FOR PASSWORDS

As a rule, it is not a best practice to ask employees or job candidates for their social media passwords. Six states have passed laws against the practice. Congress even stepped into the fray, introducing the Password Protection Act of 2012, but it was not approved by Congress.[9]

According to a June 2012 study by Workplace Options in which 31 percent of respondents worked for a company that had a social media policy, 89 percent of respondents stated that employers have no right to demand personal social networking passwords; 68 percent of respondents said that forcing employees to hand over passwords to their personal accounts would harm employer-employee relations.[10]

"Companies should protect themselves and their employees by setting clear expectations on proper social media use in the office," Dean Debnam, chief executive officer of Workplace Options, stated in a news release.[11] "However, employers must be cautious of how far they take these regulations. While social media policies themselves are not a problem, survey results show that employees do not support any intrusive measures, such as demanding access to passwords."

Such demands may actually be in violation of the federal Stored Communications Act.

"With the recent increase in technology and social media use, we anticipate more and more employees will be using social media at work, and more companies will begin creating social media policies," Debnam added. "It will be important for employers to be mindful of the guidelines put in place, striking a balance between necessary regulations and intrusive demands."

Several states have or are in the process of passing laws banning employers from asking applicants and employees for their social media passwords (see Figure 11.1). Employers are also prohibited from disciplining people for not complying with password requests.

By January 2013, six states in the United States had passed laws prohibiting employers from asking employees and job candidates for their social media passwords.

In early 2013, lawmakers reintroduced the Social Networking Online Protection Act (SNOPA). The act, which first surfaced in early 2012, would make it illegal nationwide for employers and schools to ask for social media passwords.

Figure 11.1   *Source: Compiled from news reports.*

POLICIES SHOULD ALSO ADDRESS...

Whether employers will use social media to screen candidates or employees and the inherent risks that entails. In spring of 2013, SHRM unveiled new research showing that 57 percent of companies do not have a policy relating to screening potential employees' social networking sites. Of those that do have a policy, 21 percent prohibit the use of the sites and 21 percent allow use. SHRM's research from 2011 revealed that most HR professionals—66 percent—do not Google or sift through their candidates or employees' social media sites.[12] Why? Because they are fearful they may discover something they are not supposed to know. In 2008, 54 percent of HR professionals surveyed by SHRM said they did not screen candidates by looking at their social networking sites because they were concerned about the legality of doing so; in 2013 that number rose to 74 percent.[13]

For example, employers may discover something on Facebook about an individual's protected status under federal, state, or local law (their age, gender, religion, race, political affiliations, national origin, disability, sexual orientation, etc.). Or they may discover something that state laws prohibit them from knowing about employees' activities when they are not at work. About 28 states and the District of Columbia have laws that protect applicants from employers who may discriminate against them for engaging in lawful activities (like smoking).There is the danger, too, that information found online may be untrue (fake profiles) or that employers may not be consistent when checking social media sites for all candidates. Of course, there may be exceptions—for example, if a candidate's job is working with social media. Then, a third-party could scrutinize those accounts instead of, say, a hiring manager (make sure compliance is upheld as stipulated by the Fair Credit Reporting Act).

Whatever the decision, define which employees or candidates will have their social media presences checked, when they will be examined (during a background check for example), and what information will be scrutinized. State that only publicly available information will be reviewed—and do not ask for passwords (more on that below). Being consistent is essential.

About 29 percent of organizations planned to implement formal policies governing the use of social networking sites to screen candidates by the end of 2011, up from 11 percent in 2008, according to SHRM research. By 2013, that number had decreased to 28 percent (see Figure 11.2).[14] Only a small number—30 percent—said they disqualify candidates based on information they found on social media, and 27 percent said they allow job candidates the opportunity to explain questionable information.[15]

Employers must be mindful of complying with federal record-keeping laws and e-discovery and archiving regulations for certain industries (think health care, pharmaceutical, and the financial services industries). Before investment advisors, for example, can participate in social media activities, their firms may want to make sure they have the IT infrastructure in place to capture social media data

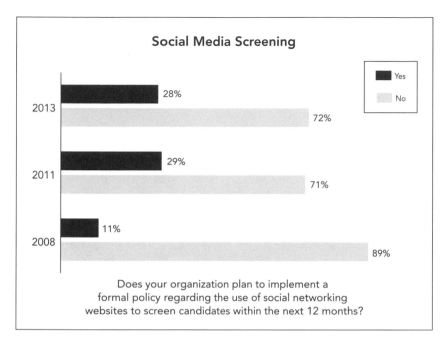

Social Media Screening

Figure 11.2 *Source:* SHRM, *Social Networking Websites and Recruiting/Selection,* 2013.

that makes sure those employees are complying with strict federal disclosure regulations. Certain industries will have to develop guidelines and the infrastructure to address how they intend to ensure employees refrain from posting content not in compliance with the law and that their firms are compliant with laws governing social media scrutiny, preservation, and e-discovery. Just in case they are sued over social media posts.

Although more than half of organizations monitor social media, only 23 percent collect and analyze data from interactions with customers, according to recent Gartner research.[16]

Consistent company branding (for example, Twitter handles could all contain the same name and an employee's first name); employer monitoring of social media accounts, ownership of those accounts generated by employees that help further the company's brand, and whether the account is company property or the employees' and whether the employee can notify followers of his or her departure without consent. Rules concerning copyright infringement; retweeting, posting, or sharing someone else's handiwork without giving them credit; and ownership of a social media account after someone leaves the company should be addressed. So, too, should the use of company logos or copyrighted material on personal accounts; endorsements of company products in non-work-related forums with disclaimers addressing an employee's employment; recommendations on LinkedIn, Facebook, Twitter, Quora, or other social sites as personal and not the firm's opinion; and which specific topics for specific stakeholders are acceptable and which topics are taboo for nonstakeholders should be addressed within the policy as well.

Consider, however, as of January 2013, there were no federal laws giving employers the contractual right to force departing employees to turn over their social media accounts or to require them to delete all social media connections made during the course of their employment.

"The law in this area has not developed nearly as quickly as the technology or the number of ways in which employees use social media," Amy Hartwig and Steven Nigh, attorneys with Michael Best in Milwaukee, told *SHRM Online* in mid-2012.[17] "Therefore, lawyers and employers are left to speculate as to what may be legally sufficient to establish exclusive control and ownership in social media sites."

Attorneys recommend employees sign agreements stating that:

- "The Twitter, LinkedIn, or Facebook account belongs to the employer and not to the employee.
- The employee is posting to the account on behalf of, at the request of, and in connection with his or her employment with the employer.
- The employee understands that, upon termination of employment for any reason, the account will stay with the employer and not follow the employee."[18]

Even if these rules are introduced, attorneys say there is no assurance that employers can claim the accounts once an employee leaves. Organizations may want to consider, too, how the accounts are used. For example, it may be plausible that a Twitter account belongs to a company if multiple employees are posting from the account. But if a Twitter account has a person's photo on it and that person tweets a mixture of business and personal information to both professional and personal connections—is that really a business account? What about LinkedIn, which contains an individual's curriculum vitae?

Now that you have laid out the strategy and designed a policy that supports it, it is time to introduce it to employees.

TRAINING IS IMPORTANT

SHRM's 2011 *Social Media in the Workplace* survey revealed that 73 percent of employers do not provide social media training to employees engaged in social media outreach to external audiences.[19] Twenty-seven percent of employers do provide social media training.

"The survey data show a disconnect in that most organizations use social media to reach audiences (68 percent) yet few train employees to effectively do so," said Mark Schmit, former vice president of research at SHRM and now executive director of the SHRM Foundation.

What should that training entail?

Although managers, supervisors, or HR professionals administering policy can use Google Docs and other platforms to reduce the number of meetings and to foster collaboration, social media trainings should accompany the introduction of the policy to encourage best practices and responsible use of social media by employees.

In addition to what can and cannot be divulged, employees who engage customers, clients, and members as themselves on behalf of their companies should be encouraged to make use of social media in a variety of ways to deliver that training, too.

> "Departments can hold brainstorming sessions or maintain ongoing conversations with questions and answers on a blog; teams can use wikis to manage projects, hold Twitter chat discussions called 'tweet chats,' share best practices and research case studies; the CEO can keep a blog or record a podcast or video; and organizations can immediately deliver news to employees.
>
> "Collaborative technologies seem to be valuable in the workplace because of their effectiveness in improving understanding and teamwork, building relationships and

developing lateral communication. The novel aspect of social media is their conversational tone: Knowledge sharing takes place through processes including discussion with questions and answers (online forums), collaborative editing (wikis), or storytelling with reactions (blogs).

"Because this is a relatively new territory for workers and their employers, many questions still exist about how these tools should and should not operate in the workplace.

For employers, the key questions are how to get business benefits out of these platforms and how to ensure that employee use of social media while at work is neither distracting nor potentially harmful to the organization," according to SHRM's website.[20]

Companies can successfully meet the goals of their social media strategies, speak to their target audiences, and keep proprietary information and data secure—if their social media policies are plain, simple, direct, and concise

But do not just give employees the policy and let them read it.

"Part and parcel with any policy, you have to have some form of training and education because you can't always trust that everyone's going to read the policy," said Eric Meyer of Dilworth Paxson LLP.

BEST PRACTICES FOR SOCIAL MEDIA POLICY & TRAINING

In addition to the above tips, some social networking policies can also include elements to make certain that:

- A social media team is assembled to collaborate on the policy's creation. The team should be comprised of people from throughout the organization who can help set the standard for social media use that accomplishes the company's objectives and goals. Given that this team will essentially be social media trainers, make sure they are given research materials, access to external training conferences, webinars, study guides or books designed to enhance their knowledge of social media as it will apply to your firm's social media strategy.

- The social media team can also serve as advisors for those staff members who need additional guidance.
- The policy is not a static document. It may have to be revised as laws change, use morphs, or new platforms are introduced, or existing ones expand. SHRM reports on such changes all the time.
- The policy outlines the company's policies as it relates to social media use by your entire staff, not just those who use it in an official capacity.
- The policy clearly and succinctly educates employees of social networking's benefits as well as its pitfalls.
- The policy covers the legal consequences for employers and disciplinary ramifications for employees, up to and including termination if rules are not met.
- Although managers and supervisors or HR professionals administering the policy can use Google Docs and other platforms to reduce meetings and foster collaboration, in-person social media trainings where conversation occurs should accompany the introduction of the policy to further encourage best practices and responsible use of social media by staff.
- Employees know they can be held accountable for content they post on the Internet—whether they are in the office, at home, or on their own time—particularly if something they post or share violates other company policies.
- The policy both conveys that employees are not to divulge trade secrets or confidential or proprietary information and also provides examples of violations of the policy.
- Employees understand expectations surrounding their productivity in conjunction with their social media habits.
- The policy guides employees on whether they need approval before posting certain types of information and tells them from whom to get approval.
- Convey to employees that they are essentially emissaries of your corporate brand because what they write on social media sites may be disseminated to the world—even if they only share it with their closest "friends."

- Encourage employees to think twice before posting comments they would not speak out loud or that they would not want their CEO, spouse, significant other, or grandparents to see. For example, we here at SHRM encourage employees to consider not tweeting when they've been drinking.
- Lastly, remember, *you are not the social media police*, rather partners in social media engagement.

12 | Making It Fit

In Don Tapscott's book, *Grown Up Digital*, he outlines the typical day of a Millennial who begins her job at 9 a.m. and does not finish until the wee hours of the morning.[1] Not that this schedule is ideal. But the point is younger people are finding ways in which to fit their work into their lives.

> **Fast Fact:** Eight-seven percent of employees in the United States say workplace flexibility is extremely or very important when choosing a new job.
> —Families and Work Institute

In her book, *Renegades Write the Rules*, Amy Jo Martin said she left her job with the Phoenix Suns as its first director of digital media and research not only to start a social media consultancy but to have three things her boss told her she could not: A career, a life, and a family.[2]

"I didn't buy it," she wrote. "Neither should you."

Social media, with its ability to connect anywhere, anytime, from any place can help employees blend work into their lives. It has certainly given me the flexibility to tap the wisdom of my peers whenever I am able, making me more productive. In fact, this book was written with insight and information gleaned not just from my investigative skill and research from SHRM, but from my social media network, which consists of my colleagues, peers, sources, and friends.

Balancing your life and your work is a misnomer. There really is no such thing.

"The word balance implies that everything has to be perfectly in sync and equal, like a balance beam or a scale . . . and that's not necessarily advantageous or possible," Ellen Galinsky, co-founder of the Families and Work Institute (FWI) told me during a telephone interview in early 2013. "Each of us prioritizes what's important at any given moment."

What you can do is manage your time—all of your time—more wisely. That is the real key in figuring out how to bring order and structure into your life—especially if you and your employees are living in a world consumed by social media distractions.

The other thing you can do is to trust your employees to do the jobs for which they were hired.

For example, I have nearly a dozen apps, including e-mail, sending notifications to my smartphone daily. When I am on deadline (or writing a book about social media for example), I need to concentrate. That means I need to prioritize, plan my day, and minimize distractions (which includes muting my phone) or carving out time in my schedule specifically to write. It also means that I may fit work into my personal time, at night, on weekends, or even on vacation, which means I may approach and talk to colleagues and sources around the clock on Twitter, Facebook, LinkedIn, Instagram, or even GetGlue. I may also need the flexibility to be able to handle other things during weekdays like doctor's appointments or my son's band recital. This approach is what works for me as a knowledge worker. Depending on their responsibilities and the natures of their jobs, of course, your employees should be allowed the freedom to get their work done in ways that work for them. Remember, those employees who fail to keep track of their time and manage that time productively might be employees whose issues with time management should be addressed.

Having mobile access to social networking sites has helped thousands of workers and netted companies billions of dollars in productivity. According to the Mobile Work Exchange, despite the security risks that mobile devices present, mobility brings significant productivity savings—95 percent of respondents to *The 2013 Digital Dilemma Report: Mobility, Security, Productivity—Can We Have It All?* say their work has improved as a result of having access to mobile devices.[3]

Mobile users gain an average of nine hours a week in estimated productivity, equating to $28 billion in productivity gains," the study pointed out.

The best way for employers to maximize the benefits social media can provide is to understand that allowing employees flexibility can lead to more engaged and productive employees.

In its 2013 report, *Leading in the Human Age*, Manpower stated,

> "Successful companies will create flexible workforce strategies aligned to their business strategy in order to boost productivity, build resilience and drive business results— even in changing circumstances. In short, this period of 'certain uncertainty' requires new approaches to the world of work."[4]

Moreover, at least one study found not embracing flexibility may likely lead to disengagement and could impede employee health.

In its *National Study of the Changing Workforce*, FWI stated that "employees' physical and mental health, stress levels, sleep quality and energy levels all significantly impact important work outcomes of interest to employers, such as engagement, turnover intent and job satisfaction."[5]

For example, the 2008 study continued, "35 percent of employees who rate their current overall health as excellent are highly engaged in their jobs, compared with only 25 percent, 22 percent, and 27 percent of employees who rate their overall health as good, fair or poor, respectively."

Galinsky co-founded FWI nearly 25 years ago to address the growing concerns of employees desiring more control over where they worked, when they worked, and their power to take time off to meet personal and family needs.

What used to be virtually unheard of back then—workplace flexibility—has now become an expectation among Millennials, particularly for knowledge workers, who literally have technology (and work) in the palms of their hands 24 hours a day.

"You've got a generation of millennials that are entering the workforce today who have been using social networking since it started," John Greer, senior consultant at JA Greer Associates in Houston, told me during an interview with *SHRM Online*.[6]

Yet, "we expect those people to be working on a BlackBerry, working at home, working at night, getting e-mails or instant messages at three in the morning and doing work for us, and yet we don't expect them to be able to access their social networks at work," said Greer, who once served as vice chairman of the International Association for Human Resources Information Management (IHRIM). In an interview with SHRM, he likened limiting access to social networks on company computers to corporate's initial reluctance to let employees have Internet access during the Internet's infancy in the 1990s.

Best-selling author Dan Tapscott refers to these Millennials as the "Net Generation"—those born between 1978 and 1997. With their 24-hour, palm-in-the-hand access to technology and all the benefits and distractions they can provide, members of the "Net Gen" have influenced the world of work, and that includes using social media to get work done. "My research shows that companies that selectively and effectively embrace Net Gen norms perform better than those that don't," Tapscott told me when I interviewed him for *HR Magazine* a few years ago.[7] "In fact, I'm convinced that the Net Gen culture is the new culture of work." He said the ways in which this generation works "turn out to be the key indicators of high-performing organizations in the 21st century."

Those indicators include the flexibility to manage one's own time and get work done. Today's employees use the Internet at work not just to do their jobs but to "recharge or eliminate boredom," Tapscott said. "Most visit social networking sites, catch up on news headlines,

Google, IM with friends, or watch videos on YouTube several times a day. Many perceive that taking a 'virtual coffee break' for 10 minutes allows them to return to their work even more focused. They don't view such activities as abusing the system."

Neither should employers.

"Far too many executives make no effort to learn from young employees. Too often, young people go to work and hit a wall of corporate procedure and a deeply entrenched hierarchy," Tapscott said. "The widespread banning of Facebook at work is a classic example of misguided supervision. The Net Generation wants to take a digital break; Boomer employers shut them down."

And when that happens, disengagement can occur, but being flexible can help employers reap rewards. So, too, can bringing this Facebook-type behavior into the working environment as evidenced by the many companies taking this approach to spark conversation and innovation.

FLEXIBILITY AT WORK IS NOT JUST A FAD

Workplace flexibility means giving employees control over when, where, and how they perform their work and permission to take time off to meet personal or family obligations and developing workplace policies that support those goals.

In 2008, approximately 43.5 million Americans served as unpaid caregivers to a family member over the age of 50. Nearly one-fifth of employed people were caregivers who provided care to a person over age 50.[8]

In 2011, SHRM and FWI began Moving Work Forward, a partnership aimed at inspiring organizations to start flexible workplace initiatives and to design guidelines aimed at increasing employee productivity and engagement to improve recruitment and reduce turnover costs.

In announcing the partnership, SHRM CEO Henry "Hank" Jackson said:

> "The global marketplace is creating new demands on business to recruit top talent from around the world, to understand and navigate competing cultures, and to be flexible enough to respond to challenges and opportunities on a 24/7 schedule. That means creating more flexible work environments that give people greater autonomy to decide how, where and when they do their best work."[9]

Using social media to gives employees new options in how they communicate with one another.

MAKING IT ALL FIT

So how does one manage all the day-to-day interruptions that come from managing social media distractions, e-mail, children, and day-to-day life?

Prioritize

Do you know which times of day you are most productive? What day of the week? Are you more productive in the office or in your studio? Do you telework? Are you more productive curled up in bed in pajamas with a laptop and smartphone? How about sitting at a desk in your home office or on your porch? Consider when and where you have done your best work. Apply it.

For knowledge workers, work is not often where you are; it is what you do, and what you can do whenever you can do it. Social media, with its ability to connect us to answers from our peers can allow companies to monetize the best of intelligence—only if employees are given the flexibility of designing how they work and when.

Structure

There is something to be said for task management tools that allow us to order our days—no matter where or when we are working. A schedule can help. Determine what your style of structure is.

"Some people like to move from their personal life to their work life and back and forth," Ellen Galinsky said. "Some people like things compartmentalized and input boundaries around the ways in which they work."

Boundaries

Focusing on the task at hand and deciding when and whether to answer e-mails, for example, can ease pressures and bring peace of mind.

Employers should discuss and decide with their staffs social media etiquette and expectations. For example, police reporters often rotate weekend shifts so one person is not always covering a shooting on a Saturday night. Social media directors should not expect to drop everything to handle a crisis anytime, anywhere. Scheduling's important. No matter the job function, be clear about who handles what, how, where, and when. Establishing boundaries early can minimize confusion and the feeling of being overwhelmed later.

Fast Fact: Most Americans online use at least one social networking site.
—Pew Internet & American Life Project

MORE TIPS FOR FINDING NIRVANA AT YOUR DESK[10]

- Do what matters most to you (the most common casualty of an excessively busy life).
- Do not spread yourself too thin—you must choose, you must prioritize. To do both well and be happy, you must say, "No thank you," to many projects, people, and ideas. "Cultivate your lilies and get rid of your leeches."
- Create a positive emotional environment wherever you are: When the emotional atmosphere is less than positive, people lose flexibility, the ability to deal with ambiguity and complexity, trust, enthusiasm, patience, humor, and creativity. When you feel safe and secure, you feel welcomed and appreciated, you think better, behave better, and are better able to help others.
- Find your rhythm: Get in the "zone," follow your "flow"—research has proven that this state of mind elevates all that you do to its highest level. When you find your rhythm, you allow your day to be taken care of by the automatic pilot in your brain, so the

creative, thinking part can attend to what it is uniquely qualified to attend to.

- Invest your time wisely so as to get maximum return: Try not to let time be stolen from you or let yourself fritter it away—use the Time Value Assessment to guide you in what to add, preserve, cut back on, and eliminate.
- Do not waste time screen sucking (a modern addiction—the withdrawal of looking at a computer/Smartphone/etc. screen): Break the habit of having to be near your computer at all times by changing your environment or structure—move your screen to a different room; schedule an amount of time you are allowed to be on the computer; plan mandatory breaks.
- Identify and control the sources of distraction in your environment.
- Delegate: Delegate what you do not like to do or are not good at if you possibly can. Your goal should be not to be independent, but rather effectively interdependent. You do for me, and I do for you—this is what makes life possible.
- Slow down: Stop and think. Ask yourself, what is your hurry? Why wake up, already impatient, and rush around and try to squeeze in more things than you should, thereby leading you to do all of it less well?
- Do not multitask ineffectively (avoid frazzling): Give one task your full attention. You will do it better. You may eventually get so good at it that your conscious mind can attend to other aspects of the task other than menial ones. This is the only way a human can multitask effectively.
- Play: Imaginatively engage with what you are doing. This will bring out the best part of your mind, focus you on your task, and make you more effective and efficient.

Appendix
Social Media Resource Guide

The intention of this appendix is to help guide HR professionals and people managers toward resources that will help them understand social media sites and how to better navigate them.

As with any topic, each person comes to social media with his or her own depth of knowledge, so for some readers, this chapter may be either one of two things: Too broad or too narrow. In addition to providing a quick overview of some social sites, this chapter by no means encapsulates them all (see Figure A.1). Remember, more social networking sites (like Snapchat, Sonico, Kik Messenger, Vine, IRC-Galleria, BizNik, Viddy and dozens of other social business sites like, IBM Connections, Socialcast, and IGLOO,) are cropping up all over the world every single day.

For example, people can use a plethora of websites to enhance their social media engagement—from sites that help you obtain a vanity Facebook URL to sites that help you schedule tweets. Dozens and dozens of nifty resources are available.

SOCIAL NETWORKING SITES: A QUICK LOOK @ THE SOCIAL WEB

Facebook

Most people know the tale of Facebook's founding in 2004 by Harvard University student Mark Zuckerberg. The site has more than a billion members worldwide and continues to grow every day. Its popularity, coupled with the birth and astronomical use of hand-held computing devices has changed the ways we communicate. According to "Always Connected: How Smartphones And Social Keep Us Engaged," a study IDC and Facebook unveiled in March 2013, 70 percent of those with smartphones use the Facebook app on their phone, second only to e-mail.[1]

In just over a decade social media has changed the way the world communicates and companies do business. What started with Live Journal and Blogger back in 1999 rapidly spawned Facebook, LinkedIn, You Tube and Twitter. And in an economy of innovation epitomised by the mantra, Fail Fast, these, along with hundreds of other start-ups, have created a multi-billion dollar social media economy.

Navigating all the disruption and business transformation can be hard, which is why we've created this map of the social media world, a group of interconnected island nations dedicated to commerce, engagement, analytics, social business, gaming and influence, centered around the mythical but fertile land of Platformia. Keep following the growth of the social media economy with our reporting at www.socialmediainfluence.com

Figure A.1   Used by permission.

Many of us would like to think that when we post something to Facebook it remains private. But in an era when someone can simply cut and paste your post, print it out, create a screen grab or copy it, we really need to redefine the notion of what privacy on social networking sites means. Your posts are only as private as the people you trust to keep them private. After all, how many times have you ever asked your Facebook friends *not* to share something you've shared on your wall with anyone else?

Facebook's Social Graph. In early 2013, Facebook unveiled its own search engine—of sorts. Called Graph Search, the site will eventually allow users to search for people, interests, photos, and places within its boundaries much in the same way Google allows users to search specific sites, such as *The Washington Post*, for example, by typing a colon after the search term ("wapo: inauguration" generates all content published within the *Washington Post*'s site on that topic). Social Graph is a little more intuitive. Based on information shared with friends, each person sees different results.[2]

· 👍 ·

Keeping It Private on Facebook

From the Facebook homepage or the timeline, click the lock or the oversized asterisk next to the word "Home," to adjust or select privacy settings. Under "Privacy Settings and Tools," personal Facebook page users can select "Who can see my stuff?" and "Who can look me up?"

Under "Who can see my stuff?" users can choose with whom to share everything they post to Facebook by selecting such options as "Public," "Only Me," "Friends," or "Custom," which allows users to share posts with selected individuals (or to block posts from being seen by selected individuals).

I won't go into a detailed description of how to set up your privacy restrictions. You need to do that. I will say this: read each choice carefully, and revisit the privacy settings from time to time because Facebook frequently makes upgrades.

Users should take note, too, of who can see what items that apps are posting to their walls or sharing in their friends' newsfeed. Let's say you are using *The Washington Post* Social Reader, and the app is instantly broadcasting everything you read in *The Washington Post* to your newsfeed for everyone on Facebook to see—including those colleagues you friended—with a date and time stamp. Given that most people do not limit who sees what when they sign up for an app, it is a good idea to check the privacy settings of the apps you use so it's not sharing everything you are doing on the app with everyone on your Facebook page—unless that is what you want.

Again, read the Facebook privacy settings to figure this out.

Many of these apps default to "Public," also known as the whole world.

One key thing to note is that you can choose to share public posts with those who "subscribe" to your Facebook page. They can see what you share publicly but will not be added as friends and see your customized status updates, photos, or places where you check in. Facebook states, "You can have broader conversations about public topics and keep personal updates for friends."

Again, Facebook makes changes often, so check your privacy settings often.

••

YouTube

YouTube was created in 2005 by Steve Chen and Chad Hurley and quickly became the Internet's TV station. Billions of people all over the world create, share, and watch videos. YouTube reports that 48 hours of video are uploaded every minute to the site, "resulting in nearly eight years of content uploaded every day." It continues to rival Google as a search engine, which is probably why Google acquired it in 2006—reportedly for $1.65 billion. YouTube users, including corporations, have used the site to set up channels for business and pleasure.

Twitter

Founded in 2006 by Biz Stone, Jack Dorsey, Noah Glass, and Evan Williams, Twitter, the social networking site that allows people to communicate in 140 characters or less, said it has grown to more than

200 million active users who generate more than 340 million tweets per day in more than 20 languages. According to the Pew Internet & American Life Project, as of December 2012, some 16 percent of online adults used Twitter, and 8 percent used it on a typical day.[3] Businesses can find primers on how to use Twitter at https://business. twitter.com. Best practices for using Twitter can be found online.

Twitter is used primarily in the United States, (62.14 percent) the United Kingdom (7.87 percent), Canada (5.69 percent), and Australia (2.8 percent).[4] Twitter said, "It's like being delivered a newspaper whose headlines you'll always find interesting."

Google+

Google+ launched in 2011 as a direct rival to Facebook and functions much in the way that Facebook does. While Facebook allows users to customize lists of people to share certain things with, Google+ calls its customization lists "circles" where users can share select information with designated groups. Touting more than 500 million members by winter of 2012, its users can use video "hangouts" to chat with up to nine people or groups of friends.[5] Users can choose to "hangout on air" and get a video of the conversation—viewable later—by adding their YouTube accounts.

Google+ users can add people, celebrities, photographers, and the pages of companies and topics to see what they are sharing publicly. At the top of the page, users can choose which circles they would like to interact with by selecting from "all," "friends," "family," or "more" ("acquaintances," "fans," or make up their own circles). Keep in mind, Google states, "When you share posts, photos, profile data, and other things with 'your circles,' you're sharing with all of your circles, except the ones you're just following."

LinkedIn

LinkedIn dubs itself as the "world's largest professional network" or, as recruiters like to call it, the single biggest resume database in the world. Founded in 2002 by Reid Hoffman, the site had grown to more than 200 million members in more than 200 countries by the beginning of 2013—66 percent of its members reportedly live outside the United States. The site reported in 2013 that "approximately two members per second join LinkedIn." Little wonder—in March 2012 LinkedIn ranked as the 31st most-visited website worldwide, according to comScore.

LinkedIn users can do so much more than just post their resumes, get references, or make introductions on the site. Users can join groups related to their expertise, or collegiate experience, or interests, ask questions, and pose answers based on those experiences and position themselves as experts. Recruiters are using the site to source passive candidates, too.

Instagram

Instagram was founded by Kevin Systrom and Michel "Mike" Kriege in 2010. A photo-sharing tool for Apple and Android devices, users can upload and change their photos by choosing a "filter to transform the look and feel of the shot into a memory to keep around forever," the site states. They can choose to share those photos on Facebook, Twitter, Foursquare, or the blogging site Tumblr. Users can comment on each other's photos and public photos within Instagram on its news feed or popular pages and can decide photo by photo whether to share those pictures across the other aforementioned networks. Keep in mind that all photos are public by default, so users must adjust their privacy settings with care. More details on using the platform can be found in Instagram's "About" section. Instagram said it has more than 30 million members in its community. Facebook purchased it in April 2012 for $1 billion.

Pinterest

Pinterest describes itself as "a content sharing service that allows members to 'pin' images, videos and other objects to their pin boards." Think virtual scrap book. The site was founded in 2011, and by mid-2012 it reportedly had more than 13 million unique visitors weekly.

Lawyers who are acquainted with copyright laws caution corporations from using the site to "pin" photos for which they have no rights. That means if you do not own the photo or do not have permission to pin it, do not pin it. By January of 2013, Pinterest absolved itself of liability regarding photos in a disclaimer on its site. "We are building the best service we can for you but we can't promise it will be perfect. We're not liable for various things. If you think we are, let's try to work it out like adults."[6]

Jonathan Pink, an attorney with Bryan Cave in Santa Monica, California, told *SHRM Online* that "the copyright issues that arise include both direct and indirect infringement under the Copyright Act."[7]

"Pinterest just makes it so easy, without even requesting uploads (like Instagram or Facebook), that the infringement can happen instantly and unthinkingly," Jonathan Ezor, assistant professor of law and director of the Institute for Business, Law & Technology at the Touro Law Center in Central Islip, New York, added."[8]

Pink said, "Absent permission from the author, or unless the work is in the public domain, anything taken—or even re-pinned—will constitute an infringement of the author's exclusive rights to reproduce and distribute that work." This information is important for because organizations may be held liable if their employees are unwittingly pinning the intellectual property of others on behalf of their companies—without getting permission first.

Myspace

Remember Myspace? Founded in 2003 and launched in 2004 the first "place for friends" grew exponentially, with a million people joining 30 days after it opened. The *Huffington Post* reported that at one point more people in the United States were visiting Myspace than Google and Yahoo combined.[9] Today, it is known primarily as an entertainment site, where young adults—the Generation Y set—can socialize and discuss "music, celebrities, TV, movies, and games that they love," according to the site, which was relaunched in 2012 under the direction of Justin Timberlake.

Foursquare

Foursquare uses global positioning systems that allow smartphone users to broadcast their locations to their friends by "checking in" from wherever they happen to be—church, the movies, restaurants, the gym. More than 20 million people were using the site worldwide in April 2012, and they have conducted more than 2 billion check-ins. Millions more check-ins are recorded daily, the site reports. More than 750,000 merchants use the location-based social networking site that allows them to offer users prizes and discounts for checking in. It was launched by its founders, Naveen Selvadurai and Dennis Crowley, in 2009. People can broadcast their check-ins to Facebook and Twitter, too, if they desire.

GetGlue

GetGlue describes itself as the social networking site for entertainment and as a former entertainment editor it is one of my favorite social networking sites. Users can earn coupons and stickers if they "check in" with their friends and followers. They can then broadcast their activity in real time on the site and externally to Facebook or Twitter and tell people what TV shows or movies they are watching, books they are reading, music they are listening to, video games they are playing, or topics they are thinking about, such as the death of a celebrity or some other significant event. It was founded in 2009 by Alex Iskold, the firm's CEO, and by January 2012 it had more than 2 million users, its PR manager Claire Gendel told me in an interview

Quora

Quora is for questions. Launched in 2010 by Facebook alumni Charlie Cheever and Adam D'Angelo, users can position themselves on the site as experts on various topics, from the serious to the mundane. It collects questions and answers to various topics and lets its 180,000 monthly active users (as of May 2012, according to AppData, an application traffic tracking service[10]) collaborate on questions and answers. For example, according to the site, "Quora delivers you answers and content from people who share your interests and people who have first-hand knowledge—like real doctors, economists, screenwriters, police officers, and military veterans." According to comScore.com, in June 2012 the site had more than 1.5 million visitors.

Imgur

Founded by Alan Schaaf in 2009, Imgur describes itself as an imaging sharing site, where users can "share photos with social networks and online communities, and [it] has the funniest pictures from all over the Internet." According to its site, users can post and share photos from across the web and use the captions to create a photo blog. They can create and manage photo albums and list images within their profiles. AppData reported that by May 2012, Imgur had 30,000 monthly active users, and those users can see how many people have viewed certain images.[11] It is likely that the same copyright rules may apply for employees sharing photos for work purposes.

SHRM Connect and HR Talk

Housed within SHRM's website, SHRM Connect (founded in 2008) and HR Talk are where HR professionals meet.

Founded in 2001, HR Talk, which was incorporated into SHRM Connect, is a bulletin board where HR professionals can have confidential discussions about HR matters. These are two examples of niche communities that continue to grow in popularity. "They use the site to make connections with other HR professionals to get their questions answered, build their knowledge of HR issues, and pose and answer relevant questions," said SHRM's manager, social networking & online communities Anne-Margaret Olsson.

"I think they're beneficial because a lot of HR professionals work alone at small and medium-sized companies and they sit in offices all day and don't have people to talk to," she said, pointing out that a lot of HR issues are stressful issues. It is nice to talk to people who can relate and commiserate as well as collaborate and share information, she added. SHRM has more than 250,000 members, and portions of SHRM Connect are open to anyone who wants to use it to collaborate, much in the same ways people do on other social networking sites.

Yammer

Yammer is a private social networking site that corporations leverage as a collaboration tool. It pretty much mimics the elements of Facebook and Twitter—but is used in a secure environment. There, employees with verified corporate e-mail accounts can share photos, files, videos, laud each other, post events, conduct polls and exchange messages and other documents. Companies own the data, which can be backed up and downloaded, and the tool is deployable from web browsers on a desktop or mobile device or through an app.

Used by more than 200,000 corporations worldwide, Yammer was founded by David O. Sacks and Adam Pisoni. Launched in 2008, Yammer states on its website that it is "among the fastest growing enterprise software companies in history." It grew to more than 4 million users in three years, and according to its website, companies like Deloitte, Ford, Nationwide, 7-Eleven, Orbitz Worldwide, Rakuten, and Telefónica O2 have adopted Yammer. So, too, has SHRM.

Dozens of enterprise social networking sites exist (more are created every day). Right now, these tools are not widely adopted for use within businesses, but they are transforming the way people work. Tools are already emerging that allow employees to work within their social media streams where they will share not only photos and videos but documents, slide show presentations, PowerPoints, to-do lists, calendars, spreadsheets, have chat discussions and conversations over instant messaging. They will collaborate on a broader scale, blasting across silos and departments. The workplace will be democratized.

In an interview with *HR Magazine* in October 2012, Steve Boese, an instructor at the Rochester Institute of Technology and host of the HR Happy Hour online radio talk show, and a longtime user of these tools, said executives are "looking for ways to extract business value from social technologies. Think about business issues first, and then talk about technology second."[12]

Some early enterprise social networking sites include Telligent, Chatter, Clarizen, Clearvale, IGLOO, Jive, Liferay, Mzinga's OmniSocial, SharePoint, Socialcast, and Socialtext. But this list does not include those companies that have built their own enterprise collaborative social networking sites—such as Deloitte's Facebook-like D Street.

"It does make a difference in employee performance and retention," Doug Palmer, principal, Deloitte Consulting LLP and the company's social business practice leader, said of his company's use of private social networks. "When you think about transforming the way you work, the ability for any of our employees to access any of these tools [helps them stay connected] in a very broad way," he told me during an interview for this book. "You don't have to be in the office to be connected. It's not the way everybody works, but we've gotten the ability to do stuff we couldn't have done two or three years ago. It gives people the flexibility to work differently."

Second Life

Second Life is an online multiplayer role-playing environment where people construct avatars to represent themselves in a 3-D virtual platform. Developed by San Francisco-based Linden Lab in 2003, Second Life has grown from being used for sometimes-risqué purposes to being used for functional business needs.[13]

In the early 2000s, companies flocked to Second Life for meetings, to stage corporate recruiting events, and to hold job fairs. By 2007, however, many companies began to abandon the spaces they purchased and branded for corporate use largely because some corporations found little use for them.

But Second Life has experienced resurgence in business use. Lately, some HR professionals have been using it to train employees and are encouraging their companies to use it to interact with customers and clients—especially those who live and work remotely.

"It's definitely an easy distribution channel," said IHRIM past chair Nov Omana, CEO and founder of Collective HR Solutions, an HR consultancy.[14] "It is appealing, intuitive and easy to use."

Zynga

If a social networking site is described as one in which people can chat and collaborate and exchange ideas and information, then Zynga, and the many games the company produces, certainly qualifies as one. Mark Pincus founded the company in 2007 "with a mission of connecting the world through games," Pincus wrote in his blog.[15]

People have reportedly met their spouses[16] on Zynga, and there is potential for collaboration in innovative ways by playing the many games such as FarmVille, Mafia Wars, Zynga Poker, Slingo, Café World, Scramble, Draw Something, and the ever popular Words with Friends. Millions of people use the Facebook apps (in May 2012, FarmVille alone had 21 million monthly users on Facebook). In all, Zynga has 232 million monthly active users; 60 million daily active users are gaming not just through Facebook, but through Android phones, Myspace, the iPad and iPhone, Yahoo, and FarmVille.com. In June 2012, game maker Electronic Arts announced that it was unveiling SimCity Social for Facebook, where players can pretend to be mayors of their own cities. When it launched Sims Social in 2011, 30 million people per month played it, eclipsing FarmVille—for a short time.

But the games are not just for fun. According to Zynga's website, "players have raised more than $10 million for several international nonprofits since Zynga.org launched in October 2009. Players have purchased virtual social goods within games like FarmVille, FishVille, Mafia Wars, and Zynga Poker that have benefitted earthquake victims in Haiti and school lunch programs for children in Haiti."

There are dozens of social networking sites. Some are here today and gone tomorrow. Remember Friendster? It was a social gaming site as recently as spring of 2012, but it was "game over" for the site by early 2013.[17]

The Others, Briefly

Snapchat, an app created in 2011 by Evan Spiegel and Bobby Murphy, allows users to take and send pictures and video that self-destruct (à la *Mission Impossible*) after a viewer opens them. According to the company's December 14, 2012, blog, 50 million "snaps" are sent daily.

Tens of millions of people were reportedly using Viddy by 2013, a sort of Instagram for video lovers. On the site, users can edit videos, share on other social sites, follow friends, and discover videos, too.

Posterous Spaces was founded in 2008 and acquired by Twitter in March 2012. According to its site, in May 2012 there were 15 million monthly users. Much like Path (launched in 2010 with more than 2 million users by May 2012), the site allows people to share privately with fewer people. "With Posterous Spaces, you control exactly who can see the contents of your website. Share with the world or with a select few—it's up to you," the site claims. A social media site for artists and lovers of art deviantART was founded in 2000 and in 2012 touted itself as the "largest online social network for artists and art enthusiasts with over 19 million registered members, attracting 45 million unique visitors per month." Tagged, which launched in 2004, is the "social networking site for meeting new people" and states it has more than 300 million members worldwide and 20 million monthly visitors. Orkut is Google's other social networking site, with most of its 34 million visitors living in Brazil, according to comScore.com.

There are social networking sites for moms (CafeMom); sites that allow you to create your own social networking sites (Ning); sites that compile all of your social networking activities in one place (about.

me); sites for people who want to meet in person (Meetup, Badoo, my-Yearbook); sites for tech folks (GitHub, Gitorious, code:keep, Ohloh, Ruby on Rails); sites for doctors (DoctorsHangout.com; Sermo), scientists (LabRoots), and even those who volunteer (Personify.it); and IndustryPigeon.com, a social networking site for industrial trade professionals.

The point is new ones come—and go—every day.

VANITY URLs—WHAT'S IN A NAME?

Some sites allow users to create their own "vanity" URLs. According to Facebook, users can customize their profiles or pages by visiting www.facebook.com/username and following the instructions.

LinkedIn, too, allows users to customize their URLs. For example, mine is www.LinkedIn.com/in/aliahwright.

To get yours, go to the settings page. In the "Privacy" box at the bottom of the page, select "edit your public profile." In a box labeled "Your Public Profile URL," select "customize your public profile URL," then type in the name of the desired URL.

Google+ does this as well for well-known brands, people, and organizations. Google+ users see a series of numbers when they go to their Google+ profiles. In 2012, the site announced it was preapproving vanity URLs for well-known, verified brands like businesses and organizations, but reportedly you have to get verified first or wait until you see the blue "claim" URL tag on your profile before you can do so.

USING TWITTER

Did you know Twitter was founded on a mobile device? This is why Twitter users are limited in the number of characters they can use to communicate. Think of Twitter like a text. You have to keep your tweets to 140 characters or fewer.

Recognize the Signs

The easiest way to understand Twitter, perhaps, is to dissect a Twitter message. Here is one constructed for this purpose:

RT @1SHRMScribe Follow @SHRMSMG to learn more about #socialmedia innovations. #SHRM members and #HR professionals @weknownext

1. "RT" means "retweet," that is, repeating someone else's twitter message. RT @1SHRMScribe means someone retweeted this message I sent (1SHRMScribe is my twitter handle).

2. @SHRMSMG is a reference to SHRM's Director of Social Strategy and Engagement Curtis Midkiff. (@SHRMSMG is his Twitter handle.) The @ symbol directs messages to him and alerts him that something has been written about him. He can see what messages have been directed toward him by clicking on the @Connect button at the top of page on www.Twitter.com, then selecting "Interactions and Mentions." This is how he can see who either mentioned him in a post or has followed him.

3. @weknownext is a reference to SHRM's public relations campaign "We Know Next." You can follow it on Twitter to get the latest HR news, trends, tips, and innovations.

4. The # symbol means "hashtag." It was created by users and is the conversation reference for any conversation. People typing in #SHRM, for example, are looking for discussions about SHRM. So anyone looking for or following tweets about SHRM or human resources will see them—if the hashtag (#SHRM for example) is placed in the search box at the top of the Twitter page. When tweeting about something you want SHRM members to see, type #SHRM at the end of your post.

5. When tweeting, users can send one-on-one or private messages directly to a person. On www.Twitter.com, go to the top of the page, click the symbol that looks

like a round gear (it's next to a quill on the right of the page) and select "Direct Message." This way, you will not make a mistake and send it out to the world. Of course, if you are going to send a message to the world, exercise good judgment.

6. Do not tweet anything you would not want your CEO, your firm's legal counsel, your grandmother or your spouse to see. (Think: U.S. Rep. Anthony Weiner. Google the CNN video: "What was Weiner thinking?")

7. When you select Direct Message, a box will pop open. Click "new message," and then type in the box at the top the Twitter handle of the person you want to reach Beneath that is another window where you can send a message—in 140 characters or fewer.

8. Only the person addressed, you have to be following each other, however, can see the message. Example: "@SHRMSMG what conference session are you moderating at #SHRM13?" Is a message to Curtis that only he can see. #SHRM13 is the hashtag for SHRM Annual Conference in Chicago in 2013.

9. Keep in mind, people make mistakes. Be careful what you say and what you RT! In general, do not retweet any links that you have not clicked on first— so that you do not send out spam or worse, a virus. A good best practice is to Google the topic of the tweet before clicking the link (time consuming, I know), but at least this way you can tell if the link is a legitimate source before you tweet it. No need to shorten links with such sites as bitly or Ow.ly. Twitter will shorten the link for you online and allow you space to continue your conversation. If someone follows you, click on that person's photo and read his or her bio to determine whether you want to follow that person or not. Remember, anyone can see your followers (including advertisers and business clients) and can decide what

judgments to make about you depending on the people you follow and vice versa.

10. On Fridays, Twitter users promote the people whose messages they follow by using the hashtag #followfriday or #ff followed by the @ symbol and the person's Twitter handle.

Looks confusing, right? Here is an explanation:

Thanks for connecting! #ff these folks: @1SHRM Scribe @SHRMSMG @SHRM_AMO @SHRM. Make sure the @symbol is right next to the handle.

Remember, follow people back! Retweet things you think your followers might find interesting. You can add them to lists and "favorite" their tweets, too. People like that. Engage people; do not just tweet inane things to them (like where you are or what you are eating—save that for Foursquare). Share things you think they will find interesting.

Keep an open mind.

Social Media Today listed a number of Twitter abbreviations.[18] Among them: MT for Modified Tweet and +1 for Google Plus.

TWITTER COMPANIONS

A number of platforms allow users to manage their Twitter feeds, Facebook posts, and other sites. HootSuite and TweetDeck are two. Crowdbooster is another. Depending on the device you decide to use to access Twitter—Android, iPad, iPhone, BlackBerry—each has a Twitter client or platform. Some help you figure out which users are more influential than others, and some not only help you schedule tweets and Facebook postings but tell you the best times of day to send them.

Google Analytics allows users to see how the data on their web traffic is used by visitors and how to make them return. And yes, it offers reports for social media sites, too.

From Radian6 to Sprout Social, literally dozens of social media monitoring tools exist—far too many to put in this book. Generally, the tools let users eavesdrop or monitor social media conversations so they in turn can engage customers, monitor their brands, and turn those discussions into tangible action items (or nip bad publicity in the bud).

There are many, many tools for smartphones and computers alike that help users manage and analyze their social media engagement. The following list is not exhaustive. More new tools are unveiled every day.

OTHER SOCIAL MEDIA TOOLS

The functions of these tools may vary depending on the device from which they are launched.

- For example, BaconReader—is an application or app for Android smart devices that organizes posts from Reddit; Baconit is the app for Windows Phones; iReddit is the app for iPhones; Reddit in Motion is the version for BlackBerry.
- Basecamp—allows users to manage projects and collaborate online all in one place.
- Bottlenoseapp—is a social listening and analyzing tool marketers employ to track conversations about brands across social networking sites.
- Brat rapid annotation tool—lets users annotate text online.
- Bufferapp—In addition to providing analytics, this tool lets users automatically direct articles, photos, and videos to their social media accounts through the day.
- Commun.it—a Twitter community management tool.
- Connectedhq—works like a digital address book with social media integration.
- Crowdbooster—Can help you manage Twitter, Facebook, LinkedIn, or other social media posts. It, too, allows users to schedule their posts, but it also provides analytics with "suggestions and tools to help you improve your online presence."
- Dropbox—a file sharing tool.

- eGrabber—a data extraction tool that helps build lists and places them in a database.
- Evernote—a note-taking tool for the web and for smart devices.
- Flipboard—lets users create their own magazines filled with news and social media sites.
- FrostWire—a free peer-to-peer network that allows users to share large files—even on their mobile devices.
- Google Alerts—daily e-mail updates based on current and relevant Google search queries.
- Google Hangouts—live video chat rooms for single or group conversations that can be preserved on YouTube if desired.
- HootSuite—A dashboard that allows multiple users to manage multiple Twitter accounts and is primarily used by teams of people who are using Twitter for strategic purposes—such as advertising campaigns or for public relations purposes. Much like Crowdbooster allows users to schedule tweets.
- IFTTT—described as "a service that lets you create powerful connections with one simple statement: IF This Then That." It was in beta in January 2013.
- Keyhole.co—described as "a real-time tracker for all social conversations around keywords, hashtags and URLs."
- Klout—this tool uses a proprietary algorithm to measure online social influence online.
- Kred—allows users to see a visual compilation of their influence on social networking sites.
- Kurrently—describes itself as "a real-time social media search engine." It scours social media sites for content.
- Listly—helps users curate the web on their sites.
- ManageFlitter—a Twitter client that helps users determine who their active and inactive followers are.
- MarketMeSuite—a social media marketing dashboard that helps companies monitor the social web in real-time for brand management purposes.
- Mylearningworx—a training tool for online learning that lets users share their expertise and find experts, too.

- Nimble—a social media-based customer relationship management system.
- NutshellMail—a tool that helps companies track their brands across social networking sites and provides summaries via e-mail.
- PeerIndex—a tool that helps users measure their online social media influence.
- Postling—a tool that compiles all of your social media sites in one place.
- Rapportive—works with Google's Gmail to show you details about your contacts' connections to social media sites.
- RebelMouse—basically builds a newspaper of your social media sites.
- Reppler—a site which allows you to manage your reputation online.
- Salesforce.com—allows companies to monitor discussions on Twitter.
- Scoop.it—a social media magazine users can create based on topics they select.
- Sendgine—a project management tool that aggregates social web content, to-do lists, files, etc.
- Sharedby—former Visibli, helps users analyze the engagement generated by what they share through social media.
- SlideShare—a service that lets users to host slide decks online.
- SocialBro—more than a Twitter dashboard, this tool helps users analyze and manage Twitter.
- Socialmention.com—another social media search engine.
- Springpad—an online organizational tool for aggregating content from across the web.
- Sprout Social—a social media monitoring and management tool.
- Storify—an online tool that lets users "discover meaningful social media from the best storytellers online, including journalists, bloggers, editors and people like you," according to its site.
- Topsy—this, too, is a real-time social media search engine.
- Triberr—a tool that claims to help bloggers grow their audiences.
- TweetChat—this tool helps users manage real-time tweet chat conversations.

- TweetDeck allows users to manage their Twitter streams or feeds. Let's say you want to follow #SHRM and #HR and #WorldSeries, #weknownext, and #Election. Just type in those hashtags and follow conversations related only to those topics. Allows you to filter conversations.
- TweetLevel—a tool that allows users to see how much buzz their brand is getting on Twitter.
- TweetSeeker—a Twitter search tool that claims to filter relevant and interesting conversations.
- Twimbow—another Twitter client.
- Twylah—helps users create websites and widgets out of tweets.
- Vizify—this tool allows you to curate a visual resume by incorporating elements from LinkedIn, Twitter, Facebook, Instagram, Foursquare, and other sites. You can see mine here: http://bit.ly/10mKUnU.
- XeeMe—this tool allows users to manage their entire social presence in one link.
- Yoono—another aggregator that allows users to compile all of their social networks and instant messaging services in one space.

Endnotes

Any missing citations may be attributed to interviews the author conducted with dozens of senior HR professionals, human capital consultants, recruiters, marketers, academics, researchers, social media experts, and Internet professionals during the preparation of this book. The author wishes to thank immensely the book's content editor, Curtis Midkiff, SHRM director of social strategy and engagement, as well as all of those individuals the author interviewed in person or via phone, e-mail, Skype, Twitter, LinkedIn, SHRM Connect, and Facebook for their expertise. This book would not have been possible without the exhaustive research and analysis extrapolated from existing content penned by the author as well as the writers and editors for *SHRM Online* and *HR Magazine*, as well as numerous studies related to technological advances, social media, and employee engagement.

Chapter 1

1. Eva Del Rio, interview by Joseph Coombs. Expert Q&A, Eva Del Rio, president and founder, HR Pro on Demand.2011, SHRM Research. http://www.shrm.org/research/surveyfindings/articles/docu ments/2011 % 20social % 20media % 20survey % 20- % 20del % 20 rio % 20q % 20 % 20a % 20jc.pdf

2. Anonymous, comment on "Topic: Social Media," HR Talk (online forum), March 2, 2012, http://apps2.shrm.org/www/forums/posting. asp?postingId = 446407.

3. @hmvtweets, Twitter post, January 2013, http://twitter.com/hmv tweets.

4. Aliah D. Wright, "HR Struggling with Facebook Snitches," SHRM, April 10, 2012. www.shrm.org/hrdisciplines/global/articles/pages/ facebooksnitches.aspx.

5. Andrew Malcolm, "Obama Speechwriter Photographed Groping Hillary Clinton Likeness," *Los Angeles Times*, December 5, 2008, http://latimesblogs.latimes.com/washington/2008/12/obama-favreau.html.

6. Helen A.S. Popkin, "Twitter gets you fired in 140 characters or less," MSNBC.com, March 23, 2009, www.nbcnews.com/id/29796 962/ns/technology_and_science-tech_and_gadgets/t/twitter-gets-you-fired-characters-or-less/#.UVHE9RzOtI4.

7. Steven McCandless, "Writing on the Wall: Marine Faces Firing Over Facebook Post," Jobsite, April 11, 2012, www.jobsite.com/news/marine-faces-firing-facebook/.

8. "H.S. Teacher Loses Job Over Facebook Posting," WCVB.com, August 18, 2010, www.wcvb.com/H-S-Teacher-Loses-Job-Over-Facebook-Posting/-/9849586/11284946/-/n9pjpqz/-/index.html.

9. SHRM Research, "SHRM Survey Findings: An Examination of How Social Media Is Embedded in Business Strategy and Operations," SHRM Research, January 12, 2012, www.shrm.org/Research/Survey Findings/Articles/P ages/2AnExaminationofHowSocialMe diaIsEmbeddedinBusinessStrategyandOperationsSurveyFindings .aspx.

10. Jessica Martinez, "*NLRB v. American Medical Response:* A Rare Case of Protected Employee Speech on Facebook," *Berkley Technical Law Journal*, March 7, 2011, http://btlj.org/?p = 1111. See also Adrian Lurssen, "Complaint and Notice of Hearing," *JD Supra Law News*, October 7, 2010, www.jdsupra.com/post/documentViewer. aspx?fid = daf37177-f935-4fe0-be1f-82c65d0f2ac3.

11. Ibid.

12. Ibid.

Chapter 2

1. Cisco, "Toothpaste, Toilet Paper, and Texting–Say Good Morning to Gen Y," Press Release, December 12, 2012. http://newsroom. cisco.com/release/1114955. Emphasis added.

2. Scott Healy, "Let Go & Lead: Unproductive Fear," Gagen MacDonald, January 16, 2013, http://www.letgoandlead.com/2013/01/unproduc tive-fear/?utm_source = feedburner&utm_medium = feed&utm_ campaign = Feed % 3A + LetGoLead + % 28Let + Go + % 26 + Lea d % 29.

3. Nielsen, State of the Media: The Social Media Report (Q3) (New York: Nielsen, 2011), www.nielsen.com/us/en/reports/2011/social-media-report-q3.html.

4. Ibid.

5. Rebekka Schlichting, "Social Media Harder to Resist Than Sex," *The University Daily Kansan*, October 22, 2012, http://kansan.com/news/2012/10/22/social-media-harder-to-resist-than-sexual-urges/.

6. Emil Protalinski, "Facebook Accounts for 1 in Every 7 Online Minutes," *ZDNet*, December 27, 2011, www.zdnet.com/blog/facebook/facebook-accounts-for-1-in-every-7-online-minutes/6639.

7. Portio Research, "Portio Research Mobile Factbook 2012," Portio Research. April 2012, www.portioresearch.com/media/1797/Mobile%20Factbook%202012.pdf.

8. McKinsey Global Institute, "The Social Economy: Unlocking Value and Productivity Through Social Technologies," McKinsey Global Institute, July 2012.

9. Telligent, 2012, http://telligent.com/.

10. Experian, *2012 Digital Marketer: Benchmark and Trend Report* (Costa Mesa, CA: Experian, 2012), http://go.experian.com/forms/experian-digital-marketer-2012.

11. Google and Millward Brown, *How Social Technologies Drive Business Success* (New York: Millward Brown, 2012), www.millwardbrown.com/Libraries/MB_Articles_Downloads/Googe_MillwardBrown_How-Social-Technologies-Drive-Business-Success_201205.sflb.ashx.

12. Gagen MacDonald and APCO Worldwide, "The 3rd Annual Employee Engagement Study: Unleashing the Power of Social Media Within Your Organization," Gagen McDonald, APCO Worldwide, December 2011.

13. Society for Human Resource Management Research. "SHRM Research Spotlight: Social Media in the Workplace," SHRM Research, November 2011.

14. Keith Hampton, Lauren Sessions Goulet, Cameron Marlow, and Lee Rainie, *Why Most Facebook Users Get More Than They Give* (Washington, DC: Pew Internet & American Life Project, 2012), http://pewinternet.org/Reports/2012/Facebook-users/Summary.aspx?view = all/.

15. Facebook, '"About," https://www.facebook.com/facebook?sk = info.
16. "Statistics Summary for facebook.com," Alexa, October 2, 2012, www.alexa.com/siteinfo/facebook.com.
17. Ibid.
18. Jessica Guynn and Ryan Faughnder, "Some teens aren''t liking Facebook as much as older users," *Los Angeles Times*, May 30, 2012, http://articles.latimes.com/2012/may/30/business/la-fi-face book-teens-20120531.
19. Keith Hampton, Lauren Sessions Goulet, Cameron Marlow, and Lee Rainie, *Why Most Facebook Users Get More Than They Give.*
21. Michael J. Tresca, "The Impact of Anonymity on Disinhinibitive [i.e. Disinhibitive] Behavior Through Computer-Mediated Communication," 1998, Michigan State University.
22. Joanna Stern, "A Tweet Leads to Firings, Death Threats," ABC News, March 23, 2013. http://abcnews.go.com/m/story?id = 18794130& ref = http%3A%2F%2Fm.facebook.com%2Fl.php%3Fu%3D http%253A%252F%252Fabcnews.go.com%252FTechnology %252Ftweet-dongle-leads-firings-death-threats%252Fstory%25 3Fid%253D18794130%26h%3DoAQEuW7SSAQGs0vNBDpFQY cGsys0e1GhN7fYzI-WVrw5UKg67WVJgEAAAA%26s%3D1.
23. Jim Franklin, "A Difficult Situation," SendGrid, Inc. http://blog. sendgrid.com/a-difficult-situation/.
24. Aliah D. Wright, "To Friend or Not to Friend?," *SHRM Online*, August 31, 2009, http://www.shrm.org/hrdisciplines/technology/ Articles/Pages/WorkersAndFacebook.aspx.
25. Associated Press, "Clicking ''Like'' on Facebook Is Not Protected Speech, Judge Rules," *New York Times*, May 5, 2012, www.nytimes. com/2012/05/06/us/clicking-like-on-facebook-is-not-protected-speech-judge-rules.html?_r = 0.
26. Eve Tahmincioglu, "Gay worker claims Facebook 'like' got him fired," Today.com. April 12, 2012. http://lifeinc.today.com/_news/ 2012/04/12/11142928-gay-worker-claims-facebook-like-got-him-fired.
27. Associated Press, "Dewayne Powers, Georgia Jailer, Fired After Facebook Friend Requesting Female Prisoner," *Huffington Post*, August 14, 2012, www.huffingtonpost.com/2012/08/14/dewayne-powers-jailer-facebook-friend-request_n_1775312.html.

28. Hellen Davis, comment on "Some Employers Are Being Sued Because Their Workers Were Texting on the Job. Have You Instituted a Policy against Distracted Driving?," *LinkedIn* (online forum), October 1, 2012, www.LinkedIn.com/groups?viewMemb erFeed = &gid = 42596&memberID = 37080881&goback = %2Eg mp_42596.

29. About Klout, 2012, http://klout.com/corp/.

Chapter 3

1. Lee Rainie, *Wired Workers* (Washington, DC: Pew Internet & American Life Project, 2000), http://pewinternet.org/Reports/2000/Wired-Workers.aspx.

2. Mary Madden and Sydney Jones, *Networked Workers Study* (Washington, DC: Pew Internet & American Life Project, 2008), http://www.pewinternet.org/Reports/2008/Networked-Workers.aspx.

3. "Trend Data (Adults)," Pew Internet & American Life Project, 2012, www.pewinternet.org/Static-Pages/Trend-Data-(Adults)/Online-Activites-Total.aspx.

4. Rainer Strack et al, "Creating People Advantage 2012: Mastering HR Challenges in a Two-Speed World," (Boston: Boston Consulting Group, October 18, 2012), www.shrm.org/ResearchSurveyFindings/Articles/Documents/BCG_Creating_People_Advantage_Oct_2012.pdf.

Chapter 4

1. James Surowiecki, *Wisdom of Crowds: Why the Many Are Smarter Than the Few and How Collective Wisdom Shapes Business, Economies, Societies and Nations* (New York: Doubleday, 2004).

2. Michael Chui et al, *Social Economy: Unlocking Value and Productivity through Social Technologies* (New York: McKinsey Global Institute, 2012), www.mckinsey.com/insights/mgi/research/technology_and_innovation/the_social_economy.

3. Globoforce. "Symantec: Case Study," 2012. http://go.globoforce.com/rs/globoforce/images/symantec_CS_web.pdf.

4. You can watch Tom Aurelio discuss Applause in this video at Globo-forceInc, "Tom Aurelio-VP of Global HR, Symantec," YouTube

video, 1:33, September 18, 2012, www.youtubecomwatch?v = ApOxvN8hxVY.

5. SourceWire News Distribution, "Employees Spend More Time on Social Networks at Work than Home," July 19, 2012, www. sourcewire.com/news/73103/employees-spend-more-time-on-social-networks-at-work-than.

6. Allen Smith, "NLRB: Prohibiting Discussion of Work Investigations Unlawful," *SHRM Online*, August 2012, www.shrm.org/legalissues/federalresources/pages/nlrb-work-investigations.aspx.

7. Cisco, "Toothpaste, Toilet Paper, and Texting—Say Good Morning to Gen Y," news release, December 12, 2012, http://newsroom. cisco.com/release/1114955.

8. Aliah D. Wright, "HR Urged To Embrace Web 2.0, Social Networking Tools," *SHRM Online*, June 6, 2008, www.shrm.org/hrdisciplines/technology/articles/pages/hrurgedtoembracesocial networking.aspx.

9. Eytan Hirsch, "Generation Y"'s Values Shake Up Corporate Cultures," *SHRM Online*, June 20, 2012, www.shrm.org/hrdisci plines/technology/articles/pages/generationy.aspx.

10. Kathy Gurchiek, "Emerging HR Discipline Is Among 2012 Predictions," *SHRM Online*, December 2011, www.shrm.org/hrdisciplines/technology/articles/pages/2012predictions.aspx? homepage = mpc.

11. SHRM Survey Findings: Social Media in the Workplace, Society for Human Resource Management, (November 2011).

12. IDC and Facebook, "Always Connected: How Smartphones and Social Keep Us Engaged: An IDC Research Report, Sponsored by Facebook," March 27, 2013. https://fb-public.box.com/s/3iq5 x6uwnqtq7ki4q8wk.

13. Ibid.

14. Kathryn Zickuhr and Aaron Smith, *Digital Differences* (Washington, DC: Pew Internet & American Life Project, 2012), http://pewinter net.org/Reports/2012/Digital-differences/Overview.aspx.

15. Jim Jansen, "Online Product Research," Pew Internet & American Life Project, September 29, 2010.

16. Meredith Ringel Morris, Jaime Tevan, and Katrina Panovich, *What Do People Ask Their Social Networks, and Why?: A Survey Study of*

Status Message Q&A Behavior (Redmond, WA: Microsoft Research, n.d.), http://research.microsoft.com/pubs/154559/chi10-social.pdf.

17. See PepsiCo Video, "Gatorade Mission Control," YouTube video, 1:16, June 15, 2010, http://www.youtube.com/watch?v = InrOvEE2 v38.

Chapter 5

1. SHRM, "Social Media in the Workplace Survey Findings," SHRM Research, November, 2011, www.shrm.org/Research/SurveyFindings/Articles/Pages/SocialMediaintheWorkplace.aspx.

2. IDC, "Worldwide Enterprise Social Software Forecast to Grow to $4.5 billion by 2016," news release, June 27, 2012, www.idc.com/getdoc.jsp?containerId = prUS23567712#.URcbNaWX9I5.

3. Ibid.

4. Alan Lepofsky, "Getting Work Done with Social Task Management," October 1, 2012, www.constellationrg.com/research/2012/10/getting-work-done-social-task-management.

5. Robert Berkman, "GE''s Colab Brings Good Things to the Company," *MITSloan Management Review*, November 7, 2012, http://sloanreview.mit.edu/feature/ges colab-brings-good-things-to-the-company/.

6. See Asana in action on YouTube at AsanaTeam, "Asana: The Modern Way to Work Together," YouTube video, 2:31, November 1, 2011, www.youtube.com/watch?v = kiLCmstyDdM&list = UU2B oogM0AqwOJyoSp1S4ClQ&index = 3.

7. David F. Carr, "Asana Offers Inbox Just For Work," *InformationWeek*, June 27, 2012, www.informationweek.com/thebrainyard/news/240002825/asana-offers-inbox-just-for-work.

8. "Applebee's Waitress Fired For Sharing 'I Give God 10%' Tip Receipt," *Huffington Post*, January 31, 2012, www.huffingtonpost.com/2013/01/31/applebees-waitress-fired-god-tip-receipt_n_2591794.html.

9. Ventana Research, "Ventana Research Releases Best Practices and Research on Social Collaboration and Human Capital Management," news release, May 11, 2012, www.ventanaresearch.com/blog/commentblog.aspx?id = 3090.

10. Gagen MacDonald and APCO Worldwide, "The 3rd Annual Employee Engagement Study: Unleashing the Power of Social

Media Within Your Organization," Gagen McDonald, APCO Worldwide, December 2011.

11. Google and Millward Brown, *How Social Technologies Drive Business Success* (New York: Millward Brown, 2012), www.millwardbrown. com/Libraries/MB_Articles_Downloads/Googe_MillwardBrown_ How-Social-Technologies-Drive-Business-Success_201205.sflb. ashx.

12. Yammer, "About Yammer," (2013) https://www.yammer.com/ about/who-we-are/.

13. Aliah D. Wright, "Experts: Flexible Workplaces Should Rely on Social Media," *SHRM Online*, November 22, 2011, www.shrm. org/hrdisciplines/benefits/articles/pages/socialmedia.aspx.

14. Katti Gray, "Web Turns Working World Inside Out," *SHRM Online*, June 9, 2009, www.shrm.org/hrdisciplines/technology/Articles/ Pages/TransformingCorporateCommunications.aspx.

15. Aliah D. Wright, "Experts: Flexible Workplaces Should Rely on Social Media."

16. Gagen MacDonald and APCO Worldwide, "The 3rd Annual Employee Engagement Study."

17. Eytan Hirsch, "Generation Y"'s Values Shake Up Corporate Cultures," *SHRM Online*, June 20, 2012, www.shrm.org/hrdisci plines/technology/articles/pages/generationy.aspx.

18. Google and Millward Brown, *How Social Technologies Drive Business Success*.

19. Ibid.

Chapter 6

1. SHRM, "SHRM Survey Findings: Social Networking Websites and Recruiting/Selection," (SHRM, 2013).

2. Ibid.

3. Jobvite, "2012 Social Job Seeker Survey," Jobvite. July, 2012, http://recruiting.jobvite.com/resources/social-recruiting-reports- and-trends/.

4. Bill Leonard, "HR Slow to Embrace Social Media," *SHRM Online*, October 22, 2012, www.shrm.org/hrdisciplines/technology/Arti cles/Pages/HR-Social-Media.aspx.

5. Facebook, "Social Jobs Partnership Application Now Live," press release. Social Jobs Partnership. (November 14, 2012) https://www.facebook.com/notes/social-jobs-partnership/social-jobs-partnership-application-now-live/404492336285577.

6. Josh Bersin, "LinkedIn is Disrupting the Corporate Recruiting Market," *Forbes*, www.forbes.com/sites/joshbersin/2012/02/12/linkedin-is-disrupting-the-corporate-recruiting-market/.

7. Alexa. Statistics Summary for Pinterest, March 29, 2013, www.alexa.com/siteinfo/pinterest.com#.

8. Facebook, "Social Jobs Partnership Application Now Live."

9. Kay Calivas, interview by Joseph Coombs, "Expert Q&A: Kay Calivas, managing director, Stephen James Associates," 2011, *SHRM Research*, www.shrm.org/Research/SurveyFindings/Articles/Documents/2011%20Social%20Media%20Survey%20-%20Calivas%20Q%20%20A%20JC.pdf.

10. Aliah D. Wright, "Social Recruiting Goes Viral," *SHRM Online*, March 12, 2012, www.shrm.org/hrdisciplines/technology/articles/pages/socialrecruitingviral.aspx.

11. Ibid.

12. Ibid.

13. Ibid.

14. Ibid.

15. Ibid.

16. Ibid.

17. SHRM, "SHRM Survey Findings: Social Networking Websites and Recruiting/Selection."

18. Aliah D. Wright, "Social Recruiting Goes Viral."

19. Ibid.

20. Ibid.

21. Ibid.

22. Dave Zielinski, "Find Social Media's Value," *HR Magazine*, August 1, 2012, www.shrm.org/publications/hrmagazine/editorialcontent/2012/0812/pages/0812zielinski.aspx.

23. Jason Hill, interview by Joseph Coombs, "Expert Q&A: Jason Hill, partner, Sound Advice Consulting Services," 2011, *SHRM Research*, www.shrm.org/research/surveyfindings/articles/documents/

2011%20social%20media%20survey%20-%20hill%20q%20
%20a%20jc.pdf.

24. Ibid.

25. Ibid.

26. SHRM, "SHRM Survey Findings: Social Networking Websites and Recruiting/Selection."

27. Ibid.

28. SHRM, "EEO: General: What are disparate impact and disparate treatment?," *SHRM Online*, April 12, 2012, www.shrm.org/ TemplatesTools/hrqa/Pages/disparateimpactdisparatetreatment. aspx.

29. Keith N. Hampton et al, "Social networking sites and our lives," Pew Research Center's Internet & American Life Project, www. pewinternet.org/~/media/Files/Reports/2011/PIP%20-%20 Social%20networking%20sites%20and%20our%20lives.pdf.

30. Aliah D. Wright, "Experts: Recruiters Using Mobile Devices Must Keep Good Records," *SHRM Online*, November 12, 2009, www.shrm.org/hrdisciplines/technology/Articles/Pages/Mobile RecruitingRecords.aspx.

31. The text of the Act is available at http://www.legislation.gov.uk/ ukpga/1998/29/contents.

32. Dan Huntley, "Proceed with Caution When Recruiting Online," *SHRM Online*, July 14, 2011, www.shrm.org/hrdisciplines/technol ogy/articles/pages/socialrecruiting.aspx.

Chapter 7

1. Michael Chui et al, *The Social Economy: Unlocking Value and Productivity through Social Technologies* (New York: McKinsey Global Institute, 2012), www.mckinsey.com/insights/mgi/research/ technology_and_innovation/the_social_economy.

2. Clearswift, "Worldwide clampdown on technology as businesses overreact to high profile data breaches," news release, September 6, 2011, www.clearswift.com/news/press-releases/worldwide-clamp down-on-technology-as-businesses-overreact-to-high-profile-data-breaches.

3. Ponemon Institute, "Global Survey on Social Media Risks," Ponemon Institute, September 2011, http://webobjects.cdw.com/webobjects/ media/pdf/Websense/Websense-Social-Media-Ponemon-Report.pdf

4. Catherine Skrzypinski, "Communicating with "Weapons of Mass Distraction," *SHRM Online*, November 19, 2012, www.shrm.org/hrdisciplines/employeerelations/articles/Pages/Communicating-Employee-Distractions.aspx.

5. "$389 Million Mobile Application Security Market Set to Explode as Threats Increase Significantly," ABI Research, September 25, 2012, www.abiresearch.com/press/389-million-mobile-application -security-market-set.

6. Dinah Wisenberg Brin, "Employer Beware: Spyware Comes to Mobile," *SHRM Online*, December 13, 2012, www.shrm.org/hr disciplines/technology/Articles/Pages/Spyware-Comes-to-Mobile. aspx.

7. Ibid.

8. Ibid.

9. Aliah D. Wright, "21st Century Social Engineering Called Huge Threat to Corporations," *SHRM Online*, October 20, 2011, www. shrm.org/hrdisciplines/technology/articles/pages/socialengineer-ingthreats.aspx; Stu Sjouwerman, *Cyberheist: The Biggest Financial Threat Facing American Businesses since The Meltdown of 2008* (Clearwater, FL: KnowBe4, 2011).

10. Ibid.

11. Ibid.

12. Ibid.

13. Aliah D. Wright, "How Can HR Help Guard Against Data Breach?," *SHRM Online*, June 27, 2011, www.shrm.org/hrdisciplines/technol ogy/articles/pages/howcanhrhelpguardagainstdatabreach.aspx.

14. Ibid.

15. Ibid.

16. Ibid.

17. Ibid.

18. Ibid.

19. Ibid.

20. Dinah Wisenberg Brin, "Employer Beware: Spyware Comes to Mobile."

21. Aliah D. Wright, "How Can HR Help Guard Against Data Breach?"

22. Ibid.

23. Ibid.

24. Ibid.

25. Ibid.
26. Gartner, "Gartner Says Monitoring Employee Behavior in Digital Environments is Rising," news release, May 20, 2012, www.gartner.com/newsroom/id/2028215.
27. Ibid.

Chapter 8

1. SHRM Survey Findings: Social Media in the Workplace, Society for Human Resource Management, (November 2011).
2. Michael Chui et al, *The Social Economy: Unlocking Value and Productivity through Social Technologies* (New York: McKinsey & Co., 2012), www.mckinsey.com/insights/mgi/research/technology_and_innovation/the_social_economy.
3. Dave Zielinski, "Social Media Tools Invade the Enterprise," *SHRM Online*, January 7, 2012, www.shrm.org/hrdisciplines/technology/Articles/Pages/Social-Media-Invades-Work.aspx.
4. Michael Chui et al, *The Social Economy*.
5. You can get a look inside Marsh U. See BenBrooksNY, "Marsh U Overview," YouTube video, 1:35, February 28, 2012, www.youtube.com/watch?v = OBxD4BIzQU4.
6. Google, "The New Multi-screen World: Understanding Cross-Platform Consumer Behavior," Google, (August 2012).
7. IDC, "Always Connected: How Smartphones and Social Keep Us Engaged: An IDC Research Report, Sponsored by Facebook," March 27, 2013, https://fb-public.box.com/s/3iq5x6uwnqtq7ki4q8wk.
8. Michael Chui et al, *The Social Economy*.
9. Bersin by Deloitte, "Bersin by Deloitte Predicts Global Talent Challenges in the Face of Business Expansion Will Drive HR, Talent and Learning Needs in 2013," news release, January 8, 2013, www.bersin.com/News/Content.aspx?id = 16167.
10. David Kiron, "How Finding 'Exceptions,' Can Jump Start Your Social Initiative," *MIT Sloan Management Review*, September 5, 2012, http://sloanreview.mit.edu/feature/how-finding-exceptions-can-jump-start-your-social-initiative.
11. See Salesforce, "Service Cloud Demo Featuring Nissan," YouTube video, 4.58, n.d., www.youtube.com/user/ServiceCloud.

12. Nielsen and NM Incite, *State of the Media: Social Media Report 2012: Social Media Comes of Age* (New York: Nielsen, 2012), www.nielsen .com/us/en/newswire/2012/social-media-report-2012-social-media -comes-of-age.html.

Chapter 9

1. Henry G. Jackson, "Embracing Social Media," *HR Magazine*, December 1, 2011, www.shrm.org/Publications/hrmagazine/Editor ial Content/2011/1211/Pages/1211 ceo.aspx.
2. BRANDfog, *2012 CEO, Social Media & Leadership Survey* (n.p.: BRANDfog, 2012), www.brandfog.com/CEOSocialMediaSurvey/ BRANDfog_2012_CEO_Survey.pdf.
3. David F. Larcker, Sarah M. Larcker, and Brian Tayan, *Director Notes: What Do Corporate Directors and Senior Managers Know about Social Media?* (Stanford, CA: Stanford Graduate School of Business, 2012), www.gsb.stanford.edu/sites/default/files/documents/TCB_ DN-V4N20-12.Social_Media.pdf.
4. IBM, *Leading through Connections: Insights from the Global Chief Executive Officer Study* (Somers, NY: IBM, 2012), http://public.dhe. ibm.com/common/ssi/ecm/en/gbe03486usen/gbe03486usen.pdf.
5. Tony Hsieh. "Values and Relationships." *SHRM Online* Video (Originally posted 2011), www.shrm.org/multimedia/video/vid_ archive/Pages/110815_hsieh.aspx. Note, the website now says 2012, but this interview was put up on the site in 2011.
6. Tony Hsieh, *Delivering Happiness* (New York, Business Plus, 2010).
7. Tony Hsieh. "Values and Relationships."
8. David F. Larcker, Sarah M. Larcker, and Tayan, *Director Notes*.
9. BRANDfog, *2012 CEO, Social Media & Leadership Survey*.
10. IBM, "2012 IBM Global CEO Study," http://ibm.com/CEOstudy (2012).
11. Ibid.
12. Bersin By Deloitte, "Bersin by Deloitte Predicts Global Talent Challenges in the Face of Business Expansion Will Drive HR, Talent and Learning Needs in 2013," Press Release January 8, 2013, www.bersin.com/News/Content.aspx?id = 16167.

13. IBM, "2012 IBM Global CEO Study."

14. David F. Larcker, Sarah M. Larcker, and Brian Tayan, *Director Notes*.

15. IBM, *Leading through Connections*.

16. Dave Zielinski, "Social Media Tools Invade the Enterprise," *SHRM Online*, January 7, 2013.

17. Ibid.

18. Consider his 90/9/1 rule at BenBrooksNY, "Measuring Internal Social Media—90/9/1 Rule," YouTube video, 2:35, May 3, 2012, www.youtube.com/watch?v = UW4dY9X8QFE&feature = plcp.

19. @BarackObama, Twitter, 2013, https://twitter.com/BarackObama.

Chapter 10

1. Cathryn Sloane, "Why Every Social Media Manager Should Be Under 25," *NextGen Journal*, July 20, 2012.

2. Ronald Zornes, comment on "OK Recruiters. What Would Be the Critical Competencies Necessary for Social Media Management," *SHRM Connect* (online forum), August 20, 2012, http://community.shrm.org/shrm/communities/viewdiscussions/message?MID = 7621.

3. Aliah D. Wright, "Wanted: HR Professionals with Social Media Skills," *SHRM Online*, September 1, 2011, www.shrm.org/hrdisciplines/technology/Articles/Pages/socialmediaskills.aspx.

Chapter 11

1. Workplace Options, "Companies Should Think Twice Before Creating Social Media Policy," news release, June 5, 2012, www.workplaceoptions.com/news/press-releases/press-release.asp?id = 9AAF1BE9E12D45409F4D&title = %20Companies%20Should%20Think%20Twice%20Before%20Creating%20Social%20Media%20Policy.

2. Allen Smith, "Facebook Firing Challenged by NLRB," *SHRM Online*, November 8, 2010, https://www.shrm.org/legalissues/federalresources/pages/facebookfiring.aspx; read the details at https://www.shrm.org/legalissues/federalresources/pages/facebookfiring.aspx.

3. Robert J. Grossman, "5 Labor Relations Battlefronts," *HR Magazine*, August 1, 2012, www.shrm.org/Publications/hrmagazine/ EditorialContent/2012/0812/Pages/0812grossmana.aspx.

4. SHRM. "Culture is Everyone's Job," SHRM Video (2011), www.shrm .org/multimedia/video/vid_archive/Pages/110816_hsieh3.aspx.

5. Elizabeth Bille, "Public or Private: Crafting an Effective Social Media Policy," *SHRM Online* webcast, July 2012, www.shrm.org/ multimedia/webcasts/Pages/0612socialmedia.aspx.

6. Jude Harris et al, "The Social Media Issue," *The Global Employer*, vol. 17, no. 3 (New York: Baker & McKenzie, 2012), www.bakermckenzie. com/files/Publication/fbb96048-99a8-49f0-9d4f-f612e0bec1c0/ Presentation/PublicationAttachment/2ee3b2aa-40e1-4612-93b8-03b7ee1feddb/bk_employment_globalemployersocialmedia_ sep12.pdf.

7. National Labor Relations Board, "Protected Concerted Activity: Section 7: National Labor Relations Act," undated, www.nlrb.gov/ concerted-activity.

8. David Kravets, "6 States Bar Employers From Demanding Facebook Passwords," *Wired*, (January 2013), www.wired.com/ threatlevel/2013/01/password-protected-states/.

9. Workplace Options, "Companies Should Think Twice Before Creating Social Media Policy."

10. Ibid.

11. SHRM Survey Findings: Social Networking Websites and Recruiting/Selection, (SHRM, 2013).

12. Ibid.

13. Ibid.

14. SHRM, "SHRM Poll: The Use of Social Networking Websites and Online Search Engines in Screening Job Candidates," SHRM (August 1, 2011), www.shrm.org/Research/SurveyFindings/Articles/Pages/ TheUseofSocialNetworkingWebsitesandOnlineSearchEngines inScreeningJobCandidates.aspx.

15. Gartner Press Release, "Gartner Predicts that Refusing to Communicate by Social Media Will Be as Harmful to Companies as Ignoring Phone Call or Emails is Today," Gartner, August 1, 2012, www.gartner.com/newsroom/id/2101515.

16. Allen Smith, "Ownership of Social Media Accounts Should Be Clarified in Agreements," *SHRM Online*, June 8, 2012, www.shrm.org/LegalIssues/StateandLocalResources/PagesOwnership SocialMediaAccounts.aspx.

17. Ibid.

18. SHRM, *SHRM Survey Findings: Social Media in the Workplace* (Arlington, VA: SHRM, 2011), www.shrm.org/Research/Survey Findings/Articles/Pages/SocialMediaintheWorkplace.aspx.

19. SHRM, "Managing and Leveraging Workplace Use of Social Media," (Arlington, VA: SHRM, 2012), https://www.shrm.org/TemplatesTools/Toolkits/Pages/ManagingSocialMedia.aspx.

Chapter 12

1. Don Tapscott, *Grown Up Digital: How the Net Generation is Changing Your World* (New York: McGraw-Hill, 2008).

2. Amy Jo Martin, *Renegades Write the Rules: How the Digital Royalty Use Social Media to Innovate* (San Francisco: Jossey-Bass, 2012).

3. Mobile Work Exchange, "Alarming Number of Fed Smartphones Have Zero Password Protection," Press Release, (January 2013).

4. Manpower Group, *Leading in the Human Age: Why an Era of Certain Uncertainty Requires New Approaches to the World of Work* (Milwaukee, WI: Manpower Group, 2013), http://files.shareholder.com/downloads/MAN/2283536317x0x6   29531/26f84eaf-0ec4-4034-9eaf-18d9fb7c9015/WEF_2013_Leading_Human_Age_FINAL_20130121.pdf.

5. Kerstin Aumann and Ellen Galinsky, *The State of Health in the American Workforce: Does Having an Effective Workplace Matter?* National Study of the Changing Workforce, rev. ed. (New York: Families and Work Institute, 2011), http://familiesandwork.org/site/research/reports/HealthReport_9_11.pdf.

6. Aliah D. Wright, "HR Urged To Embrace Web 2.0, Social Networking Tools," *SHRM Online*, June 6, 2008, www.shrm.org/hrdisciplines/technology/Articles/Pages/HRUrgedToEmbraceSocialNetworking.aspx.

7. Aliah D. Wright, "Millennials: 'Bathed in Bits'," *HR Magazine*, July 1, 2010, www.shrm.org/Publications/hrmagazine/Editorial Content/2010/0710/Pages/0710wright.aspx.

8. *Work-Life Balance and the Economics of Workplace Flexibility* (Washington, DC: Executive Office of the President, Council of Economic Advisers, 2010), www.whitehouse.gov/files/docu ments/100331-cea-economics-workplace-flexibility.pdf.

9. Stephen Miller, "Workplace Flexibility Partnership to "Move Work Forward'," *SHRM Online*, February 1, 2011, www.shrm.org/about/ news/pages/fwipartnership.aspx.

10. Adapted from Edward M. Hallowell, *CrazyBusy Overstretched, Overbooked and About to Snap!: Strategies for Coping in a World Gone ADD* (New York: Ballantine, 2006). Reprinted with permission.

Appendix

1. IDC, Facebook, "Always Connected How Smartphones And Social Keep Us Engaged," IDC, Facebook (March 2013).

2. Facebook, "Introducing Graph Search," 2013, https://www.face book.com/about/graphsearch.

3. Joanna Brenner, "Pew Internet: Social Networking (full detail), Pew Internet & American Life Project, Feb. 14, 2013, http:// pewinternet.org/Commentary/2012/March/Pew-Internet-Social-Networking-full-detail.aspx.

4. Alex Cheng and Mark Evans, "Top Twitter Countries," in *Inside Twitter: An In-Depth Look Inside the Twitter World* (Toronto, ON: Sysomos, 2009), www.sysomos.com/insidetwitter/#countries.

5. Google Official Blog, "Google+: Communities and photos," De-cember 6, 2012, http://googleblog.blogspot.com/2012/12/google-communities-and-photos.html.

6. Pinterest, "Terms of Service," (2013), http://about.pinterest.com/ terms/.

7. Allen Smith, "Pinterest Might Facilitate Copyright Infringement," May 29, 2012, SHRM, http://www.shrm.org/legalissues/federal resources/pages/pinterest.aspx.

8. Ibid.

9. Timothy Stenovec, "Myspace History: A Timeline Of The Social Network's Biggest Moments," *Huffington Post*, June 29, 2011, www.huffingtonpost.com/2011/06/29/myspace-history-timeline _n_887059.html#s299557&title=July_2006_Number.

10. AppData, Independent, Accurate Application Metrics and Trends from Inside the Network, May 2012, www.appdata.com/.

11. Ibid.

12. Bill Roberts, "Social Media Gets Strategic," *HR Magazine*, October 1, 2012, www.shrm.org/publications/hrmagazine/editorialcontent/2012/1012/pages/1012roberts.aspx.

13. Aliah D. Wright, "HR Breathes New Life into Second Life," *SHRM Online*, June 9, 2011, www.shrm.org/hrdisciplines/technology/Articles/Pages/SecondLifeRevisited.aspx.

14. Ibid.

15. Mark Pincus, *Mark Pincus' Blog*, http://markpincus.typepad.com.

16. Ben Silverman, " 'Words With Friends' spells love and marriage," Yahoo! Games, January 6, 2012, http://games.yahoo.com/blogs/plugged-in/words-friends-spells-love-marriage-173817262.html.

17. Robert McMillan, "The Friendster Autopsy: How a Social Network Dies," *Wired*, February, 27, 2013, www.wired.com/wiredenterprise/2013/02/friendster-autopsy/.

18. Bliss Hanlin, "Top Twitter Abbreviations You Need to Know," (2012, May 22), *eModeration via Social Media Today*, http://socialmedia today.com/emoderation/512987/top-twitter-abbreviations-you-need-know.

Index

About the Author

Aliah D. Wright, an editor/manager for *SHRM Online*, is a subject matter expert on HR technology, social media, and digital communication trends. She began her journalism career in college working simultaneously as an editorial assistant for the *Philadelphia Daily News* and a part-time stringer for the *Philadelphia Inquirer*. After receiving a bachelor's degree in journalism from Temple University in her hometown of Philadelphia, Wright worked as a reporter and copy editor for the *Greenville News* in Greenville, South Carolina, before heading back to Pennsylvania to take a job as a copy editor with the *Harrisburg Patriot-News*. She then worked as a general assignment reporter and political correspondent for the Associated Press in Pennsylvania. She left there to head entertainment coverage for all of Gannett newspapers, including the nation's largest daily, *USA Today*, where she managed a team of entertainment reporters nationwide for Gannett News Service. She began working in SHRM's editorial department in March of 2008. In addition to writing for *HR Magazine*, she is responsible for HR technology and business leadership and strategy coverage for the SHRM website. She lives in Northern Virginia with her 13-year-old son, Jaden, an avid gamer, Dragon Ball Z expert, and aspiring theatrical music producer.

Additional SHRM Books

The Power of Stay Interviews for Engagement and Retention
Richard P. Finnegan

Proving the Value of HR: How and Why to Measure ROI
Jack J. Phillips and Patricia Pulliam Phillips

Stop Bullying at Work: Strategies and Tools for HR and Legal Professionals
Teresa A. Daniel

Up, Down, and Sideways: High Impact Verbal Communication for HR Professionals
Patricia M. Buhler and Joel D. Worden

Workflex: The Essential Guide to Effective and Flexible Workplaces
Families and Work Institute and Society for Human Resource Management